**The Rise and Fall of the Poster**
# Street Talk

This photograph was taken by Jesus Sierra near the Elephant and Castle, South London. It was inspired by Luis Barragán's Paseo de los Gigantes, Mexico City. Promenade of the Giants.

This book is dedicated to Hans & Pat Schleger and Bob Gill
for unforgettable work and memories. MF

Published in Australia in 2006 by
The Images Publishing Group Pty Ltd
ABN 89 059 734 431
6 Bastow Place, Mulgrave, Victoria 3170, Australia
Tel: +61 3 9561 5544  Fax: +61 3 9561 4860
books@images.com.au
www.imagespublishing.com

Copyright © The Images Publishing Group Pty Ltd 2006
The Images Publishing Group Reference Number: 689

National Library of Australia Cataloguing-in-Publication entry:

Frost, Malcolm.
Street Talk - The Rise and Fall of the Poster.

ISBN 1 86470 123 4.

1. Posters – History. I. Lewis, Angharad.
II. Winterburn, Aidan. III. Title.

741.674

Edited by Andrea Boekel

Design and graphic production by Malcolm Frost and Graeme Martin

© 2005 Text by Angharad Lewis on pages 40-60
© 2005 Images and text by Catherine Slessor on pages 125-130

Digital production and print by Sing Cheong Printing Co. Ltd., Hong Kong

IMAGES has included on its website a page for special notices in relation to
this and our other publications. Please visit www.imagespublishing.com

The Rise and Fall of the Poster

# StreetTalk

**Malcolm Frost | Angharad Lewis | Aidan Winterburn**

*images*
Publishing

Gerry Mitchell | Gina Moriaty 2005

# Contents

Massimo Vignelli was born in Milan. In 1957 he and his wife Lella were awarded fellowships to the United States. In 1965 they started Unimark International and in a few years had offices in America, Europe, South Africa and Australia. In the 1970s Vignelli started Vignelli Associates in New York. The Vignellis' work includes graphics, exhibition design, product and furniture design, interiors and corporate programmes. *Design is One*, was published by IMAGES in 2004 and illustrates the huge range of their work and achievement. The illustration shows Vignelli Associates' proposal for a bus shelter for JC Decaux.

## Foreword : Urban Moments | Massimo Vignelli

There is no doubt that the advent of the electronic media has somewhat largely decreased the relevance of the printed media, however, the printed media permanence has its precise role that cannot be made completely obsolete.

The strength of electronic media is its speed and ubiquity, however it requires the appropriate equipment to be retrieved. Conversely, printed matter's strength is its own presence in that it does not require any intermediate equipment to be retrieved. It is what it is: whole. The poster, a sheet of paper pasted on a wall to announce events or products, is a simple device that can hardly be efficiently or economically replaced by any other.

This book examines the poster as a medium of communication, from its inception to today, with a brilliant and clear essay by Angharad Lewis, to which I cannot add anything more relevant, nor wish to do so.

For me, the poster is a vehicle to carry information publicly in places where no other media is available. Here, the poster is alive and it performs its function. I am much less interested in commercial posters advertising a product, since printed advertising and television commercials are already saturating the marketplace.

I do not like the use of posters as mailing pieces. I cannot stand the waste of paper. However I like posters that are printed on both sides, starting as small size publications that unfold to become a poster. I think this is a very effective format; a perfect one for example, for non-profit organisation announcements, conveying information on one side and creating an impact on the other.

I do not think the poster is dead, but without doubt, its appropriateness of use has changed. With vision, its destination is enriched; with good sense its use still valid. In the hands of creative designers it could be a formidable medium, or a poetic touch to enrich all our lives.

This book analyses the current nature of posters, more evocatively than any other book so far on this subject, and I consider it an extremely important contribution to a better understanding of the public poster as part of human communication and a medium that remains potent even today.

A commission to design a poster is the best thing that can happen to any graphic designer. I started my formal design education in 1957, and I'm still working today with the same enthusiasm and joy. Nearly 50 years later, having worked on every type of print job (including the design of commemorative postage stamps), I still get my biggest buzz from designing posters. Public posters are generally big and don't stay around for very long. They are democratic and have to exist in a competitive environment and the production budgets are usually fair. Every contemporary designer is familiar with the 'art' aspect of the poster – from Toulouse-Lautrec, Leupin, Muller-Brockmann, Eckersley and so on – more so than in any other graphic problem. Work 'For the public good' is always a consideration, and to think seriously about the built environment makes a

**Stepping Out | Malcolm Frost**

NOSE

change from basically a two-dimensional business, but the greatest personal challenge for the designer is that always, in this situation, their work is put on the line. Passing traffic has to be first made aware of the poster site, has to take in the details quickly, and has then to be convinced to act in some way. I've designed, or helped to design, hundreds of posters and the concrete results (in box-office sales, attendance figures and so on) has never been taken lightly. As a designer it is impossible to disassociate oneself from the whole process – the success or failure of each piece.

The catalyst for this book came about when a long-term client explained to me that he now preferred to target customers through his company website. He found the poster flawed beyond resurrection – they did not represent value for money,

and he couldn't be sure his posters were even being noticed. Six-feet-high letters that nobody even sees.

With Angharad Lewis and Aidan Winterburn, and photographers Gerry Mitchell, Gina Moriarty, Jesus and Lucy Sierra and Paolo Rosselli we have tried to discuss and illustrate the possible demise of the public poster as an important communications vehicle. The argument for direct-market targeting is profound, the poster is now linked with 'urban-blight', the street is now frenetic and a graphic cacophony, and as we are all bombarded with unrequested information during every waking moment. We have become indifferent to 'messages' and/or commercial appeals.

The main essays in the book are supplemented by a section about the

built environment, from a graphic scale to the architectural by Catherine Slessor, and finally some students' work in response to an Images Publications competition.

The authors and contributors are all part of the design community, although from different strands of the industry, and we all agree that good design exists only for the common good. The public poster as a piece of work has been prized, collected and even framed in our homes, but it now seems to be under sentence. The design industry has evolved through substantial and constant technological and commercial change, and the fall of the poster will not be total. Nothing ever is. I would like to thank personally Massimo Vignelli for his contribution.

London, April 2005

Advertising may be described
as the science of arresting human
intelligence long enough to get
money from it.

**Stephen Leacock**
Canadian humourist

**Photograph Gerry Mitchell**
Old Street London 2004

I WOULD LIKE TO INVITE
YOU TO WALK WITH ME.

JUST FOLLOW THE LINE.

Take a walk through London and you will experience an unrelenting mass of visual communication, much of which will be in the form of posters. You will see towering 48-sheet billboard posters; posters on mechanical, rolling boards at roadsides; posters in bus shelters and on telephone boxes; fly posters smothered over buildings and bridges, in backlit frames in Tube stations and papered inside Tube tunnels; you will see them outside colleges, galleries and churches and on the sides of passing buses. There is no way you can avoid them and yet their ubiquity and familiarity means that sometimes their messages are easy to miss. In fact, although you might not know it from the average poster-lined city street, if you peel away a few layers you find that the story of posters is heading for a sticky ending. The poster is in the throes of an identity crisis and its importance as a means of communication is being seriously challenged. Under threat from targeted forms of marketing, the validity of the poster's egalitarian nature is being contested. And in the face of increasing privatisation of public space by legislation that favours the heavy weight economy of billboard advertising, the poster has become criminalised and marginalised in the very place where freedom of expression and democratic communication are most important: the street. This book unpicks the poster's inner workings, looks to its past, explores its present and finds out where the future of the poster lies.

'A dead medium' is the phrase I have encountered most when talking to designers about posters. This pessimistic (perhaps realistic) view of the poster is, however, always posited within a passionate rhetoric about the medium that would suggest it is anything but dead. People love posters. They are eminently collectible, cheaper and less intimidating to buy than fine art. There are innumerable websites selling every type of poster imaginable, and countless more books about posters and poster designers. People love collecting them

and they also love designing them. For graphic designers the poster is the ultimate end game in the problem-solving challenge of graphic design: large scale, mass communication that hones a message into snappy visual repartee.

The history of the poster is a sprawling subject, reaching into countless other areas of political, social and cultural life; from giving voice to public dissent, to providing life-saving information, to inaugurating new art movements, the poster has allowed the few and the voiceless to be seen and heard by the many and the powerful. The poster owes its democratic powers to two basic characteristics: it's versatility (posters are fast and cheap to produce) and its accessibility (they can be pasted up anywhere for all to see). The history of the poster is also, effectively, the history of graphic design and is the perfect embodiment of what graphic design is at its purest level: the composition of word and image in the service of a message. It is not restricted to commercial ends (a distinction sometimes used to delineate the boundaries between art and design) but rather by the simple need to convey an idea or body of information in the most effective way.

**The Art of Posters**
Commerciality is sometimes a factor in graphic design, as it is in art. Artists must sell work to make a living, but unlike the graphic designer, the artist's work is free to serve any or no message. As is proved by the rich history of protest posters, however, the message in graphic design can be as much about personal expression as fine art is. The poster is where art and graphic design and the practice of the individual artist and graphic designer, meet most closely. At the beginning of graphic design in the late 19th century, when it wasn't called 'graphic design' posters were the work of artists. Later, the artists of the European Modernist movements of Russian Constructivism, Dutch De Stijl, Italian Futurism and the German Bauhaus pioneered new visual vocabularies that

were used to communicate with and serve the masses, through magazines, books, architecture and posters.

The poster has always hovered between art and commerce because, despite the poster's material ephemeralness, it has, by its nature, to be visually enduring, burning an image onto our memories. For many designers the poster is an artistic medium, rather than one used merely in the service of commerce. Amsterdam-based design studio Experimental Jetset has revisited the spirit of European Modernism in a series of posters and positioned it in the bus shelters of 21st-century New York City. The designers were asked to create a remote exhibit for Terminal 5, an art exhibition celebrating the opening of the new Eero Saarinen-designed terminal at JFK airport, in Autumn 2004. The designers' response was to produce posters that on first glance appear to be conventional advertising.

Closer inspection, however, reveals that rather than selling a brand or product, these posters tell a remarkable story about the language of posters as a whole. It is not a straightforward revisitation of modernism for its own sake, but a critique on the practice of appropriating modernist visual language that began in America after the Second World War and continued to evolve alongside commercial advertising. The posters, entitled Modernism Un/Fulfilled, bring the voices of Filippo Marinetti, Theo van Doesburg and Laszlo Moholy-Nagy to the streets of Manhattan and explore how those artists' nascent visions of the future, formed in the early 20th century, have been borne out today.

'The subject of these posters,' explain Jetset, 'is something that interests us very much, which is the legacy of modernism. Inspired by the fact that the exhibition takes place in a terminal designed by Saarinen, a European

Experimental Jetset, bus shelter posters.
A remote exhibit for Terminal 5, New York.
Photography David Reinfurt 2004

modernist who lived in the US, we wanted to research the somewhat awkward relationship between pre-war European modernism and post-war American modernism. So we took three historical quotes (one Bauhaus quote, one Futurist quote, and one De Stijl quote) and transformed these quotes into 'prototypical' airline advertisements. In other words, the posters deal with the question whether the 'Americanisation' of modernism was a form of fulfilment or a form of commodification."

The issues addressed in Experimental Jetset's Terminal 5 poster project form a succinct version of the story of early 20th-century graphic design. After the First World War, European avant-garde artists began breaking with the traditional hierarchies of fine art. In order to get their message across, Futurists and Dada artists began using typography in a visual way, treating letters as images and using leaflets and posters to disseminate the idea of social and political revolution. Along with other movements – Dutch De Stijl and Russian Constructivism – these artists wanted to challenge profoundly the values of Western culture and representational art and turned for this end to abstraction, austerity and experimentation.

The German Bauhaus began, in the early 1920s to dissolve the boundaries between art and its practical application in everyday life, dedicating its artists and workshops to textile design, furniture making, architecture, advertising and publicity. These avant-garde artists wanted to communicate with the world and did so by employing mass-production and a pared-down visual language that embodied the vigour of their message and the mechanical means of delivering it. After the Second World War a Diaspora of European artists had emerged around the world, in Britain, the United States and Switzerland, where an already well-established poster design tradition now gave rise to the revolutionary and highly influential International Typographic Style. Artists in Britain and the US, who had

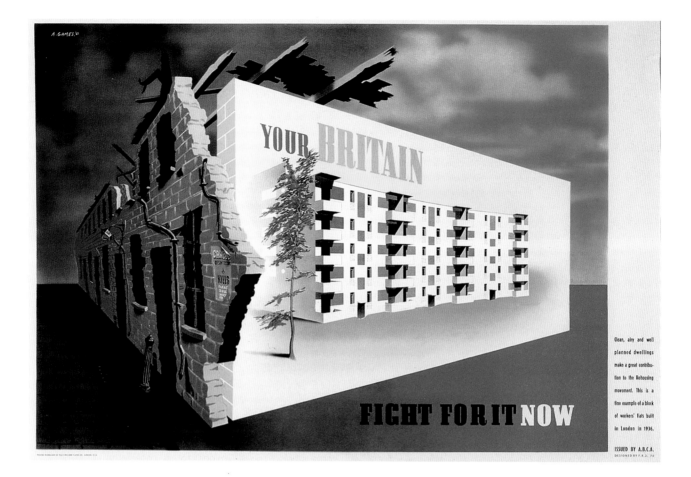

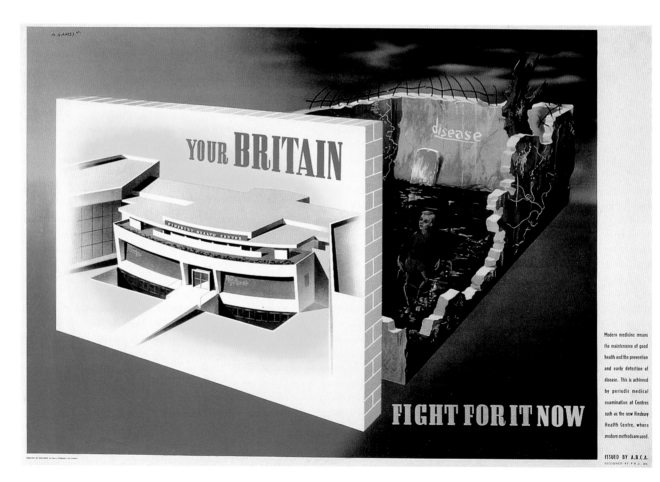

fled the anti-Semitism and persecution of artists in their native countries, contributed to the war effort by creating posters for the US and UK Ministries of Information and when the war was over they began working in the burgeoning advertising industry as post-war economies began to be rebuilt. America became a temporary home for the Bauhaus where the presence of exiles including Walter Gropius, Laszlo Moholy-Nagy and Herbert Beyer meant that a rather staid visual culture was given a shot in the arm and the new advertising industry got a kick-start in artistic and graphic innovation.

Experimental Jetset's work deals with this dispersal of European Modernism and the appropriation of its ideals and language for other ends. As Jetset explains: "It's very much about the co-modification of modernism. The posters show how easily modernism is corrupted; combine these highly ideological, even spiritual slogans with some stock photography of airplanes, and suddenly these posters are airline advertisements". Despite the fact that Jetset's posters consciously mimic the appearance of advertisements in order to make their point; and despite the fact that they are framed within a context set aside for advertisements, and posit a link between the posters and an exhibition, they are not to be seen merely as promotion for the exhibition. These are posters as art objects.

"We weren't asked to design posters advertising the exhibition", they explain, "we were actually asked to design the posters as a public space art project. On the posters, we could do anything we wanted, as long as we included the URL of the website somewhere underneath. So it was actually an art assignment. But being designers, we treated it basically as a design assignment, in the sense that the posters really refer to the context of the exhibition – airplane travel late-modernism, etc ... We're so glad we have them hanging in the streets of New York City. These absolutely have to be seen in context to get the full surreal effect. Futurists in Queens!"

Modernism Un/Fulfilled is an encouraging use of public space, indeed it is a coup for graphic design to be able to wrest back some of the space that regulated billboards and poster sites have taken over for advertising. The beauty of the poster is that, in its rightful place on the street, anybody can see it. Posters divert your attention to things you never knew existed and ideas you never considered before – they make an art gallery of the street.

**Printed Messengers**
The poster exists in many forms. The *Concise Oxford English Dictionary* gives it three definitions: 1. A placard in a public place. 2. A large printed picture. 3. A billposter. Most people would also tend to separate posters into two categories – those they would put up at home (generally prints of art or photographs) and those they would expect to see outside on the street, advertising products and events or announcing information and opinion. This book is concerned with the latter, although at times these graphic design and advertising posters, also make their way indoors, to homes, museums and art galleries. There is also a distinction between commercial, mass-produced posters and homemade vernacular posters displayed in local communities or used to voice opinions in protest marches. What unites them all is the poster's unique ability to act as a go-between connecting the public and the private. A poster carries a message from a particular source and reaches a mass audience, each individual person experiencing it on an intimate scale. There is no partiality or discrimination with posters; they do not seek to target one group of people over another but to impart their message democratically to whoever walks by. In today's new climate of targeted marketing, however, the indiscriminate method of the poster is seen as outmoded and not the most economic means of reaching an audience. But as people pass over the poster as a

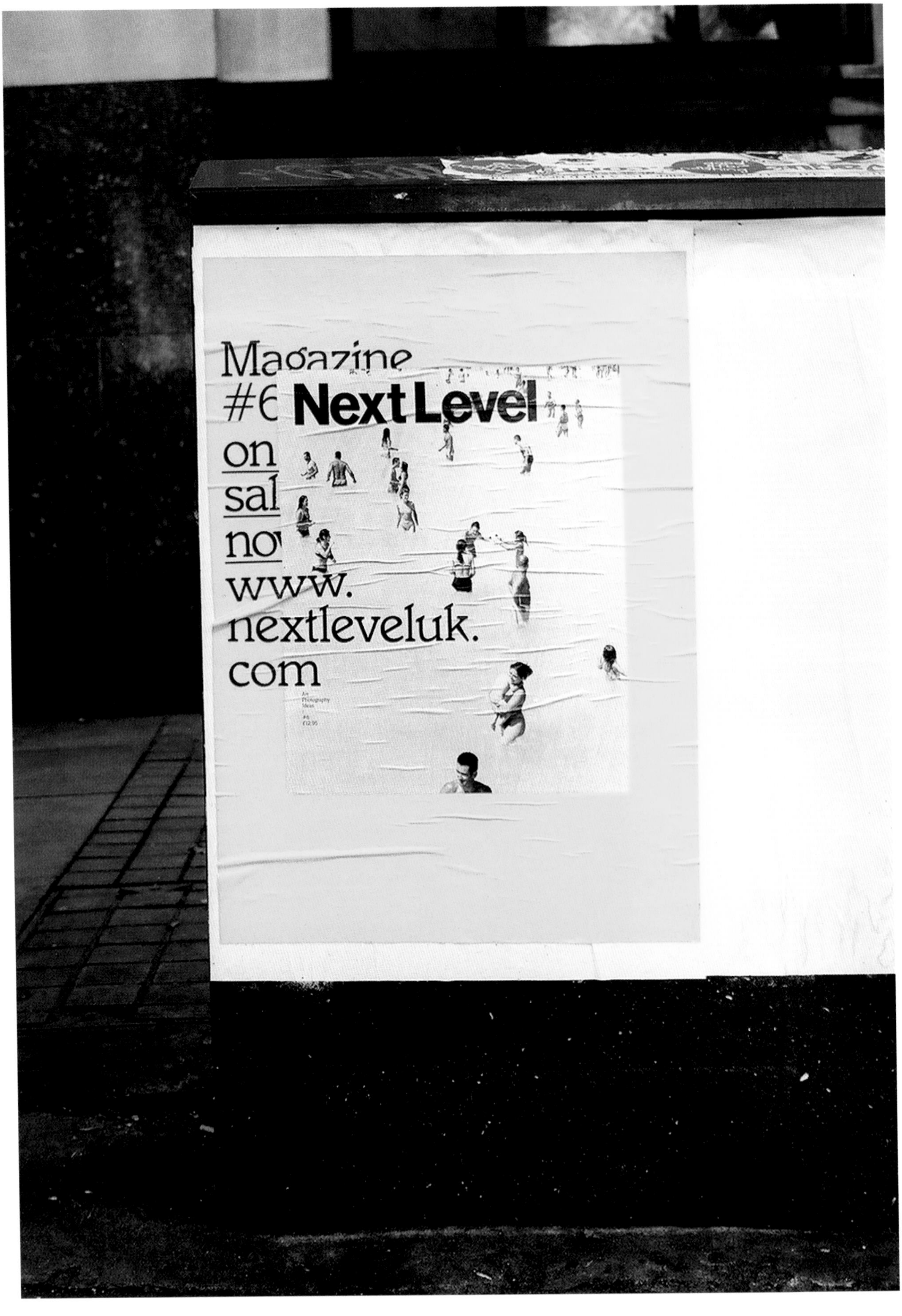
Magazine
on
www.
nextleveluk.
com
Next Level
#6
£12.95

means of communication, instead choosing direct mail, online, print and radio advertising and e-mail as a way to deliver their message, we are losing a medium that gives us a wealth of choice, in favour of directing information at us depending on our age, gender, postcode, occupation, tax-bracket or lifestyle.

One of the poster's greatest strengths is immediacy. If the definition of a 'living' poster is one that is fulfilling its primary function – that of delivering a message to the public – then once the information a poster relays is out of date, technically it dies. Fly-posters in this respect, are the most visible and vital of posters, appearing overnight in sites already blistering with other posters. They stay relevant only until the performance, single, gig, club night or issue of a magazine they advertise has been replaced by the next, and a new poster is pasted up in its wake. As objects that function in this way, posters are materially without value. The whole point is that they are cheap, fast to produce and disposable. London-based Malone Design regularly designs posters for the music industry. David Malone explains how a balance of high-visibility and cheap production leads his approach to fly-poster design: "When I'm doing a teaser campaign for one artist, I can get four posters out of one print run by changing the plates around. It's a nice way of making something quite simple go a long way. I did that for Virtual Insanity for Jamiroquai – the whole wall of the Westway was covered in every different colour permutation of the poster and it looked like the record company had spent loads of money when actually they hadn't."

The very transience of the poster also invests it with historical value. Its ephemeral nature means that despite being disposable, if preserved, it acts as a social document, creating a record of the tastes, activities, interests and attitudes of a specific people at a specific time. Once a poster has died, it gains an afterlife as a messenger in history.

We look at posters in a museum and understand something about how the world looked, what people were interested in and how they communicated in a different time.

Despite having traditionally lowly status in the hierarchy of visual culture, posters are influential within it. Writer and cultural commentator Michael Bracewell, talking at a symposium on independent publishing at Tate Modern, in Autumn 2004, cited the example of a particular poster in a discussion about the speed at which popular culture absorbs and regurgitates itself into something new; what he called 'the ever tightening coil of society'. His discourse was on the accelerating speed with which ideas and images, ways of thinking and living, are conceived, disseminated, adopted, hybridised and transformed. Cultural transfusions occur more and more rapidly, with ideas released spore-like, reabsorbed and hybridised elsewhere. Bracewell's example was *Trainspotting* by Irvine Welsh: the book is the progenitor of a new literary vernacular in the 1990s, which then produces a film, which produces a poster, which inspires a catalogue of pastiches and rip-offs. Posters are at the fore of such cultural relay races. They are not the thing or the event itself but its signifier, its remote identity, its image. Posters are like drones taking messages about a primary event, product or piece of information out to the world at large. They are immediate and expendable, produced in large quantities, inherently cheap and valueless, a many-times diluted version of the primary thing, there in its service to bloom quickly, impart the information and be rapidly replaced by a new generation. In this sense posters are analogous to bacteria, viruses and mayfly. When the information is out of date they become redundant, die and are unceremoniously plastered over by new, more relevant, younger posters. Conversely however, this invests them with value and collectibility. They begin to have value as historical documents – visual snapshots of a time and place.

Poster for the film *Trainspotting* designed by Mark Blamire and Rob O'Connor Stylorouge 1995. Photography Lorenzo Agius

Poster by Value and Service for *Next Level* magazine

MARLENE DIETRICH

*Angel*

REGIE
ERNST LUBITSCH

Marlene Dietrich
Frans Mettes 1937

Alon Levin, fly-posters for PSWAR
Amsterdam 2004 - 2005

24    Photography Alon Levin 2005

Each poster has a story to tell. There is a reproduction of a poster for the 1937 Marlene Dietrich film *Angel* (released in the Netherlands in that year), designed by Frans J.E. Mettes, in the book *A Century of Posters*, by Martijn F. Le Coultre and Alston W. Purvis. The story of this image begins with the film itself, and the image of Marlene Dietrich.

Dietrich was a film icon – the public knew her through her image and her memorable face, which came to stand for her. It appeared on miles of celluloid, countless movie screens and innumerable film posters. The way the image of a movie star like Dietrich is experienced is akin to the way posters work. Dietrich acted her role on the set of *Angel* and what the cinema-going audience then experienced was a Dietrich distilled from the original that had passed through the hands of make-up artists, lighting artists and editors, transposed onto celluloid, distributed to theatres and projected through light onto the screen: hundreds of images of Dietrich flickering in front of thousands of pairs of eyes. In the case of posters, 'Dietrich' is the product, event, service or brand.

The message can be anything; 'Visit Switzerland', 'Help the War Effort', 'Stop the War', 'Travel by Train', 'Fill up on Shell', 'Read *The Times*'. Once the message has been generated, it is handed to a poster designer who hones into a visual composition that can be digested in an instant. This image is then sent to a printer that multiplies it, creating hundreds of paper drones, carrying the distilled, visualised message: 'The New Dietrich Film is Out'. Now the posters are pasted up around the city to coincide with the film's release. People glimpse it, read it and maybe go to see the image of Dietrich flickering on the silver screen.

An image of the Dietrich poster has also ended up in *A Century of Posters*, so the story doesn't end there. Indeed, you are looking at it reproduced once again on these pages. Although Mettes' poster was designed to convey a message in a specific moment, the image of that poster still has currency today. It has been preserved and in the process it has become another kind of message carrier. The fact that posters are so time-specific and speak with such immediacy makes them innately historical once that moment has passed. As historical documents they become indicators of what we choose to remember and a reflection of our identity as well as of the past.

**Novelty in a Shrinking World**
Although the poster in its modern incarnation is widely agreed to have begun in Paris with the work of Henri Toulouse Lautrec and Jules Cheret, the antecedents of those posters have been around since humans first developed written language. In Roman times graffiti was used as a political voice box; after the advent of moveable type in the 15th century information was disseminated by the means of printed handbills and posters; during the Reformation, Martin Luther spread his teaching through publicly displayed edicts; and in the 18th century, as printing technology advanced, public notices became the most important means of communicating from the local to the national and international stage. The poster, from its most primitive form, has been the arbiter of social, political and religious change, a powerful communicator whose audience was reached at street level.

The way we communicate with each other today is vastly more complex. Our individual worlds have become at once larger and more private: we receive images and information from around the globe, transmitted to the private interfaces of the televisions and computer monitors in our homes. We even read our newspapers on-screen. In the days before television, and certainly before radio, if you wanted to find out what was going on in the world you went out of your door and down the road and if you wanted to tell the world something, this is where you posted your message.

# IMPORTANT ANNOUNCEMENT NO. 4

SOMEONE TOLD ME NOT TO BE SO NEGATIVE, I GAVE IT A THOUGHT. IS ME BEING NEGATIVE NOT A RESULT OF MY SURROUNDINGS? IS IT NOT WHAT I AM EXPERIENCING THAT DETERMINES MY STATE OF MIND? I REALISED THINGS HAD TO BE CHANGED, OR JUST BE DIFFERENT, BUT I WAS WONDERING HOW IF I AM NEGATIVE AS IT SEEMS AND MY SURROUNDINGS ARE NEGATIVE IS THERE A WAY TO MAKE SOMETHING POSITIVE. IF IT WAS A MATTER OF SCIENTIFIC PRINCIPLE IT COULD HAVE BEEN MUCH MORE SIMPLE, NEGATIVE AGAINST NEGATIVE IS POSITIVE, IT IS ME AGAINST THE VOID, OR THE VOID AGAINST ME, IT DOES NOT REALLY MATTER. I SKETCHED MYSELF A FEW POSSIBILITIES TO SEE IF I CAN MAKE SOME SENSE OUT OF IT.

I CAME UP WITH FOUR POSSIBILITIES. THE FIRST, ME BEING NEGATIVE AGAINST THE EXISTING NEGATIVE, WHICH GAVE A POSITIVE RESULT. SECOND WAS ME BEING NEGATIVE AGAINST A NON EXISTING POSITIVE, WHICH ONLY LEFT ME WITH A NEGATIVE. THE THIRD WAS THE OPPOSITE OF THE SECOND BUT STILL REMAINED NEGATIVE, AND THE FOURTH WAS UTOPIC, ME POSITIVE AGAINST A NON EXISTING POSITIVE RESULTING IN POSITIVENESS. THERE WAS NO REASON FOR ME TO BELIEVE IT WAS POSSIBLE THOUGH, AND IF IT WAS, IT MUST AT BEING HAVE BEEN TOO EASY. IT WAS THE FIRST POSSIBILITY THAT SEEMED TO BE THE CASE, OR AT LEAST I LIKED THE IDEA OF. A NEGATIVE ME ACTING AGAINST NEGATIVE SURROUNDINGS. RESULTING IN POSITIVENESS. IT SEEMED I DID NOT FIND WHAT THE VOID WAS BUT A WAY TO ELIMINATE IT. I ONLY NEEDED TO ACT AGAINST IT, AS MY ACTION COULD CAUSE A POSITIVE REACTION.

THIS WEEKEND IN **PUBLIC SPACE WITH A ROOF**, SOME PEOPLE WILL ORGANISE **WORKSHOPS** AND **WALKS** THROUGH THE CITY.
**PROGRAMMING FOR CITIES** WILL BE GIVEN BY **WILFRIED HOU JE BEK**, OF SOCIALFICTION.ORG, WHO HAS A LONG HISTORY IN DEVELOPING COMPUTATIONAL SYSTEMS WITHOUT TRADITIONAL HARDWARE. THE WORKSHOP WILL REINFORCE A LONG EXISTING LINK BETWEEN CODE AND ARCHITECTURE. **FRIDAY DECEMBER 3 FROM 3 PM YOU + ME = YOU (I AM NOT A LOT)** AGON IS A WALK ORGANISED BY **PIETERJAN GINCKELS**. HE WILL WALK THROUGH THE CITY WITH PSWAR AS A CENTRE POINT, MAKING PICTURES OF THE PATH HE WILL INFECT WITH HIS NOTES. THE WALK WILL TAKE PLACE BETWEEN THE **4TH** TO THE **11TH DECEMBER.**

**BOAZ BAR ADON** WILL INVITE PEOPLE TO FOLLOW HIS ROUTE ON **SATURDAY DECEMBER 4.** HIS IDEA IS TO MAKE A ROUTE BASED ON PERSONAL PLACES OF AN EXISTING PERSON LIVING IN THE CITY, AND GIVE THIS ROUTE BACK TO THE CITY, AND THERE AFTER TO GIVE OTHER PEOPLE THE CHANCE TO 'FOLLOW' THIS PERSON.

**INTERVENING THE URBAN VOID - PSYCHOGEOGRAPHIC DATA**
RESEARCH PROJECT ON STRATEGIES OF INTERVENTION IN THE CITY
NOVEMBER 13, 2004 - FEBRUARY 12, 2005
FOR EXACT TIMES OF **WORKSHOPS AND WALKS** SEE **WWW. PSWAR. ORG**

**PUBLIC SPACE WITH A ROOF** IS ALSO OPEN FROM THURSDAY TO SUNDAY FROM 3 TO 7 PM
OVERTOOM 301
1054 HW AMSTERDAM
THE NETHERLANDS
PSWAR@XS4ALL. NL

---

# IMPORTANT ANNOUNCEMENT NO. ♭5

ACTING WITHIN ALL THE NOISE, I FELT I WAS BOUND TO DISAPPEAR. I TRIED TO IMAGINE SILENCE.

THIS **SATURDAY** IN **PUBLIC SPACE WITH A ROOF**, MORE PEOPLE WILL GIVE LECTURES AND WORK PRESENTATIONS AND ON **TUESDAY** THEY SCREEN A MOVIE.
ON **SATURDAY DECEMBER 11**, FROM **3 PM**,
**MICHAEL BULL**, IS A SOCIOLOGIST LECTURER IN MEDIA AND CULTURAL STUDIES. HE WROTE THE BOOK '**SOUNDING OUT THE CITY**' ON THE WAYS THAT INDIVIDUALS USE PERSONAL AUDIO DEVICES (MAINLY WALKMEN) TO TRANSFORM THEIR EXPERIENCE OF URBAN SPACE. HE WILL SPEAK ABOUT THE **IPOD** AS A MEAN TO CREATE YOUR OWN PRIVATE SPACE IN PUBLIC.

**TAO G. VAHOVEC SAMBOLEC** IS A COMPOSER AND SOUND ARTIST, HE WILL SPEAK ABOUT '**REALITY SOUNDTRACK**', A PUBLIC INTERVENTION THAT TOOK PLACE IN **PUBLIC SPACE WITH A ROOF** IN 2004. THE AUDIBLE RESULT OF THE ACTION IS A MOVING CLOUD OF SOUND, WHICH IS TRAVELING THROUGH THE CITY

ON **TUESDAY, DECEMBER 7 AT 9 PM.**
**MON ONCLE**, DIRECTED BY JACQUES TATI, FRANCE, 1958.
MANUTAU ORGANISES AND CURATES THE MOVIE SERIES ON CITY AND ARCHITECTURE. HE WILL INTRODUCE **MON ONCLE** WITH A SHORT CINEMA-PERFORMANCE.

**INTERVENING THE URBAN VOID - PSYCHOGEOGRAPHIC DATA**
RESEARCH PROJECT ON STRATEGIES OF INTERVENTION IN THE CITY
NOVEMBER, 13 th 2004 - FEBRUARY, 12. 2005
FOR FURTHER INFORMATION OVER THE PROJECT AND PEOPLE SEE **WWW.PSWAR.ORG**
THE EXHIBITION AND ARCHIVE OF INTERVENING THE URBAN VOID CAN BE SEEN FROM THURSDAY TO SUNDAY BETWEEN 3 AND 7 PM.
**PUBLIC SPACE WITH A ROOF**
OVERTOOM 301
1054 HW AMSTERDAM
THE NETHERLANDS
PSWAR@XS4ALL. NL

---

# IMPORTANT ANNOUNCEMENT NO. 6

I HAD TO ADOPT A FORMAL APPEARANCE, AFTER ALL I HAD TO MAKE SURE PEOPLE TAKE MY ACTIONS SERIOUSLY. I DID NOT THINK THIS COULD HAPPEN IF I DID NOT HAVE A FORMAL APPEARANCE. AN APPEARANCE THAT WOULD BE WITHOUT A DOUBT MORE ACCEPTED. I PRINTED IT OUT, AT FIRST GLANCE I WAS HAPPY. IT FELT AS IF I MADE A BIG STEP FORWARD TO BEING RECOGNISED, I ADOPTED AN APPEARANCE PEOPLE WOULD FOR SURE NOT DOUBT. BUT AS I WAS THINKING HOW TO CONTINUE, I REALISED THAT IN THAT I HAD MISSED THE POINT. PEOPLE WOULD NO LONGER QUESTION MY CONCERNS, THEY WOULD SIMPLY BE TAKING MY APPEARANCE FOR GRANTED AND BY THAT I RISKED CREATING AN EVEN GREATER VOID, A BIG NOTHING. I MADE A CLEAR DECISION TO KEEP MY TRUE APPEARANCE, TO LEAVE IT FOR THE PEOPLE PEOPLE TO THINK AND QUESTION THE MEANING. FOR THE SAKE OF NOTHING I DREW THIS :

I WAS CONTENT, IT MIGHT MAKE SOMEONE HAPPY. IT MIGHT BE POSITIVE.

THIS WEEKEND IN **PUBLIC SPACE WITH A ROOF** IT CONTINUES WITH **CRITICAL PRACTICE/DIALOGUE**
ON **FRIDAY, DECEMBER 17 AT 7 PM**
**ORIGINALFASSUNG** PRESENTS '**TRAVEL REPORTS 3 : AMSTERDAM TRAVELOGUE**'
THEY WILL ALSO ORGANISE A SERIES OF EVENINGS AT PSWAR, AS PART OF THE PROJECT.
(DATES TO BE ANNOUNCED ON THE PSWAR SITE)

ON **SATURDAY, DECEMBER 18 AT 3 PM**
A DISCURSIVE PICNIC BY **UNWETTER** AT PSWAR - ON THE FLOOR, ON THE BLANKET. BE A GUEST, BE A HOST. IDEAS. FOOD. TALK.
**MOHAMED BENZAOUIA** AND **KOBE MATTHYS** PRESENTS THE **UNIVERSAL EMBASSY** IN BRUSSELS. MOHAMED BENZAOUIA IS THE FIRST PERSON THAT GOT A BELGIAN PASSPORT FROM THE UNIVERSAL EMBASSY.

ON **SUNDAY, DECEMBER 19 AT 4 PM**
**C-CRED** PRESENTS THE **COUNTERCARTOGRAPHY** PROJECT THE PROJECT'S ARCHIVE WILL BE SHOWN AT PSWAR.
**HEIMO LATTNER** WILL SPEAK ABOUT **ORIGINALFASSUNG**'S ACTIVITIES IN BERLIN AND ABROAD.

ON **TUESDAY, DECEMBER 14 AT 9 PM**
A FILM SCREENING WITH AN INTRODUCTION BY **MANUTAU**.
**TRON, BY STEVEN LISBERGER (USA 1982)**

**INTERVENING THE URBAN VOID**
RESEARCH RESEARCH PROJECT ON STRATEGIES OF INTERVENTION IN THE CITY
NOVEMBER 13, 2004 - FEBRUARY 12. 2005
FOR FURTHER INFORMATION OVER THE PROJECT AND PEOPLE SEE **WWW.PSWAR.ORG**
THURSDAY TO SUNDAY BETWEEN 3 AND 7 PM - THE EXHIBITION AND ARCHIVE OF INTERVENING THE URBAN VOID IS OPEN.
**PUBLIC SPACE WITH A ROOF**
OVERTOOM 301
1054 HW AMSTERDAM
THE NETHERLANDS
PSWAR@XS4ALL. NL

---

# IMPORTANT ANNOUNCEMENT NO. 8

HAVING IT ALL SUMMONED UP MEANT I COULD NOW MAKE THE NEXT STEP TO KNOWING, BUT STILL IT WAS NOT ENOUGH, I HAD TO TRY IT OUT TO KNOW THAT IT WORKS. SINCE I FEARED I WAS RISKING ANOTHER ENDLESS CYCLE I HAD TO GIVE IT A LIMITATION.

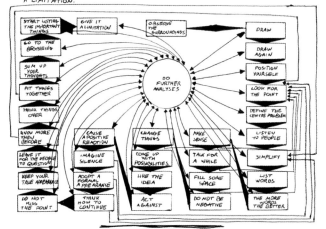

THIS WEEKEND **PUBLIC SPACE WITH A ROOF** CONTINUES WITH THE LAST RESEARCH FIELD, **URBAN ARTICULATION.**

ON **SATURDAY, JANUARY 15 AT 12 PM**
WORKSHOP CONDUCTED BY **TOY-SHOP & SWOON** ON CREATING AND MANUFACTURING STENCILS, CUT-OUTS AND POSTERS;

ON **SUNDAY, JANUARY 16 AT 4 PM**
**SWOON** FROM NYC WILL TALK ABOUT HER ONGOING PUBLIC PROJECTS, AND PRESENT HER NEW SERIES OF CUT-OUTS, DRAWINGS AND WOOD CUTS COLLECTED FROM THE ACTUAL STREET SCENES, PORTRAYING THE CITY; LIFE-SIZE
**LESLIE JULIAN STEIN** AND **POLINA GRIGORYEVNA SOLOVEICHIK** FROM **TOY-SHOP** WILL PRESENT THEIR WORK, STENCILS AND CUT-OUTS ON THE CITY'S FACADES AND CHANGES COMMERCIAL INTO PRIVATE PLACES FOR ADVERTISEMENTS;
**SIEBE THISSEN** WILL LECTURE ABOUT GRAFFITI AND PUBLIC SPACES. "WHILE THE PUBLIC SPACE EVAPORATES FURTHER AND FURTHER, TAGS MAKE THE STREET MORE AND MORE PUBLIC; HOW MUCH PUBLICNESS CAN A CITY STILL TOLERATE ?";
**MONIKA VYKOUKAL** WILL TALK ABOUT HER GRAFFITI INVESTIGATION SINCE 1993, WITH A BACKGROUND IN ART HISTORY, SHE HAS CONTRIBUTED REGULARLY TO GRAPHOTISM MAGAZINE, LONDON AND SPRINGERIN, VIENNA. SHE IS CURRENTLY ASSISTANT CURATOR AT PEACOCK VISUAL ARTS, ABERDEEN.

**INTERVENING THE URBAN VOID**
RESEARCH PROJECT ON STRATEGIES OF INTERVENTION IN THE CITY
NOVEMBER 13, 2004 - FEBRUARY 12. 2005
FOR FURTHER INFORMATION OVER THE PROJECT AND PEOPLE SEE **WWW.PSWAR.ORG**

**PUBLIC SPACE WITH A ROOF** IS OPEN FROM THURSDAY TO SUNDAY FROM 3 TO 7 PM.
OVERTOOM 301
1054 HW AMSTERDAM
THE NETHERLANDS
PSWAR@XS4ALL. NL

This is not to say that today our streets are bare however, rather quite the opposite. We absorb an ever-increasing amount of visual information, all of it competing for our undivided attention. In the scrum for attention-grabbing novelty amongst street signs, the means of communicating has outstripped the message itself. Thus we have neon signs, scrolling messages on the street and cinematic-proportion moving image screens in rail and bus termini.

Dutch designer Alon Levin believes that, in his words, 'the poster has killed itself' the visual competition among posters to monopolise the attention of the passing masses means that novelty is the norm and all posters fade into wallpaper; a patina on the surface of the street with the same effect as snow blindness. As an antidote to this effect, Levin designed a series of posters that subvert the received visual lexicon of posters. The posters were publicity for a run of lectures entitled 'Intervening the Urban Void at Public Space With A Roof (PSWAR)', an artist-run space in Amsterdam that hosts exhibitions, projects, lectures and an archive of publications and art documents related, as it describes, 'to themes of a shared public and social interest'. Levin systematically flouts all the 'rules' of poster design in this series. The text is densely set and hand written, with crossings out and mistakes intact; the copy itself does not consist of the usual title/location/date/ time structure of a lecture poster but is instead a highly personal reflection on the theme of the lectures by Levin himself, which evolves over the course of seven posters. Levin's entire approach challenges the traditional way in which the viewer interacts with posters. They can't be deciphered from a distance and their idiosyncratic appearance draws us in to an intimate proximity where they can be read (the greyscale effect of densely set text actually makes them stand out among posters utilising flat, bright colours and large, bold type). Levin's use of handwriting calls to mind the type of vernacular poster you might produce

yourself at home to find a missing cat or advertise a room for rent. Furthermore, the posters are designed to be read in instalments, with a narrative running between them. Levin asks a lot from the viewer with these posters and although only a very small proportion of people who pass them will engage with them fully – reading the entire text and looking out for the next instalment – those who do cannot fail to feel challenged, curious and, ultimately, compelled to attend the lectures. Indeed the posters, which were posted all around Amsterdam from November 2004 to February 2005, provoked some strong responses, which Levin recorded. They also cleverly invoked the subject, intervening the Urban Void, which sought to explore how artistic practices affect our interaction with urban landscapes. Levin's posters, polarise themselves entirely from advertising posters, in their assumption of curiosity and intelligence on the part of the general viewer and their rebuttal of traditional poster-design techniques.

**Graphic Design Vs Advertising**
There is an important distinction to be made between graphic design and advertising posters. The most prevalent poster you see on the street today is the advertising poster, which is conceived as one part of a larger, cross-media campaign to promote a product. It is displayed in the most prominent legal sites on the street from bus shelters to vast billboard hoardings. The graphic design poster is more elusive and tends to be seen either as a fly-poster (confined to fairly limited areas where fly-posting is tolerated, though still illegal) or doesn't make it onto the street at all. Indeed many graphic designers who make posters no longer expect them to be displayed in a street context. The cultural poster, which is perhaps the sub-genre of posters that belongs most to graphic design, is by extension, more and more marginalised in the street. Without the funds to meet the cost of space to display posters, (driven by competitiveness in the advertising industry) or pay fines meted

Alon Levin, series of fly-posters for lecture series Intervening the Urban Void, PSWAR, Amsterdam 2004 - 2005

MUSEO NACIONAL
DEL PRADO
MANE
en el Prado
14 octubre 2003 - 11 enero 2004
Venta anticipada de entradas: 902 400 222
www.museoprado.es
CREDIT SUISSE
FUNDACIÓN winterthur

out for illegal fly-posting, cultural institutions are becoming less willing or able to commission poster designers.

The difference between an advertising poster and a graphic design poster is not necessarily obvious to ordinary consumers amidst the visual noise of the street. It is also a distinction that has not always existed. As Angus Hyland, partner of international design studio Pentagram, points out, the modern poster was invented by artists and later appropriated by commerce. "If you go back to the beginning of the last century, advertising posters, posters for theatres, playbills, that kind of thing, were done by sole practitioners – artists – in gouache…" He says, "Its only when you get the birth of modern advertising that you get the difference between, say, a clearly defined poster pushing a product or brand, a soap powder or an ink pen or whatever, and posters deemed to be promotion or information-givers on cultural events."

This division is alive and well in posters today: posters promoting a brand or product are produced by the advertising industry and those which exist to promote and relay information about cultural events tend to be created by graphic designers. "Stylistically some advertisements, which take the format of posters, actually do them in a style very closely associated with those graphic design posters" continues Hyland. "It's as much to do with who actually does the poster as the content or application of the poster… Just as you have groups like Pentagram, which are clearly graphic design consultancies, you have advertising agencies that are clear where they're coming from. Although I think your consumer, your passer by, will be completely confused as to what the difference is between one and the other, other than some vague recognition of something that is beautifully designed rather than something created to push a concept and promote a product".

In today's advertising-saturated world we have become discerning about what we absorb visually. Advertisements, we know, are a confection: images of ideas of what other people think we think. We know they are there to make us buy something but advertising conspires to turn billboards into mirrors, so that when we look at them we think we are looking back at ourselves. This is an attempt to deflect and distract us from looking beyond the surface and to begin examining the story of labour, technology, economics and marketing that has led to the image being placed before us. If we were to probe behind the image in advertisements and explore this hidden story we might soon discover important things about the product being promoted that, at best, would raise an eyebrow, and at worst, make your flesh crawl.

What is missing from advertisements is the story about what happens to our cash once we have parted with it in exchange for a product: that is not a part of the process of seduction that will make us open our wallets. The ads dazzle us, stop us from seeing the void between expenditure and profit, between the owners and the workers; they tell us that we have the power of ownership too. Instead of reality, ads present us with a glossy fiction of the world with which they cajole and flatter us. The fact that we are complicit in this process, willing to absorb, unquestioned, the illusory world of advertising because it is easier than unpicking it, is a horrible realisation. Advertising is not rocket science we all know how it works but we choose to ignore the machinations behind it, preferring instead the vision of ourselves laid out in advertising. Thus the idealism proffered in advertising has become a flimsy substitute for emotional and spiritual fulfilment. Instead of something to strive for, idealism is now served up on a plate. Or on a billboard. All we need to do is part with cash to gain it, or so the advertisements intimate.

This obscures another void, that chasm between what we need and what we

Pentagram, Museo del Prado, Madrid 2004

**29**

want; what we know and what we pretend not to know. We shy away from reality to escape into our complex state of fictional existence; far removed from our human state. We attach importance to what seems to take precedence in our everyday lives: ease, convenience, speed, absolution and instant gratification, all achievable with direct debit charity donations, media-filtered humanity, point-of-sale good deeds and non-committal spirituality. Deconstructing this existence would mean a total collapse of our way of life.

Photographer Stephen Gill has explored this void in his series of photographs *Billboards*. They depict the backs of billboards around London. The titles of the photographs are derived from the slogans appearing in the unseen advertisements. The sense of bathos created by the contrast between our mental vision of the glossy idealism summoned up by the slogans and the patchy desolation depicted in Gill's photographs blows open the myth of reality in advertising.

Graphic design remains aloof from the games of persuasion and illusion of advertising because, rather than apply itself to cajoling, aspiration or guilt-inducement, graphic design deals in the more straight forward concerns of layout, legibility and type-image relationships to deliver its message. There is a sense that 'good design' prevails in cultural posters by graphic designers, while it does not in posters by advertising agencies. While a person engaged in designing advertising posters is subjected to the marketing-driven specifications of the client, the graphic designer exercises more choice, taking responsibility for the solution of how the poster's message will be delivered. Thus the graphic designer can impose his or her own rigour in layout and typography when composing a poster, while the advertising designer is part of a chain of decisions by client and account managers. The perceived design hierarchy in posters, however, is also as much to do with what the poster is promoting as who has designed it. Posters are judged

on either cultural or historical value; thus a poster for a washing powder has little cultural capital on the day it is designed but after 20 years it might have become a historical document worth examining as a missive from the past.

Nostalgia, however, is not enough to make a poster well designed. Despite the fact that there are more posters on our streets today than ever before, there will be fewer 'classics' remembered than there have been from previous eras. Quality does not come hand in hand with quantity. The last golden era of posters was with the New International style in the 1960s – a graphic evolution begun in Switzerland that had a huge impact on posters still felt today.

Tony Brook of London graphic design agency Spin, which designs posters and other graphic material for galleries including the Whitechapel and Haunch of Venison, decries the lack of vision or spending power of clients who fail to see the value of posters to promote exhibitions or products. He cites the rich heritage of posters that has, in the past, become an important part of a gallery or museum's identity and history as reason enough to encourage a gallery to promote its shows with posters. For the Museum fur Gestaltung Verlag in Zürich, the posters it has commissioned to coincide with its exhibitions over the years have become much sought after collectors' items and work just as hard at promoting the museum as its current posters. Amsterdam's Stedelijk Museum has an unrivalled heritage of exhibition poster design. Willem Sandberg worked at the museum as a director and designer from 1938-62 and created more than 270 Stedelijk posters. His influence as the Museum's director was profound but his design work had a different kind of endurance. In a book celebrating Sandberg's work published in 2004, Ad Peterson observes, "Over the years, Sandberg's museum activities and his attitude to contemporary art have been an inspiration to many in the museum world. The exhibitions he showed have

'Your money should work harder not you. Make more of your money. DWS Investments.' Stephen Gill, 2005
Part of the *Billboards* series

Pentagram, Art and Architecture 1993
Pentagram, Out of Joint Theatre Co 1995
Pentagram, The Crafts Council 1998
Angus Hyland, Don't Panic 2005

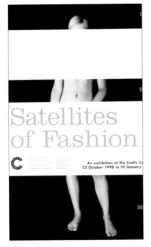

since passed into history, but his typographical work and the spirit imbued in it have stood the test of time".

In 2004 Spin held an exhibition in its studio that brought together a grouping of classic posters by modern masters including 1960s Swiss School pioneers Josef Müller-Brockmann, Karl Gerstner, Max Bill and Emil Ruder, leading Dutch designers Wim Crouwwel, Ben Bos and Benno Wissing, and British pioneers 8vo, among others. As Brook points out, it would be impossible to do a show like this of work being produced now. Although he and his contemporaries get the occasional opportunity to produce great posters, the medium does not occupy the princely position that it did in the 1960s and 1970s. That era had Crouwel's Stedelijk posters, Müller-Brockmann's work for the Tonhalle, Otl Aicher's 1972 Olympic posters and Hans Hofmann's Kunsthalle Basel posters. Even the 1980s and 1990s were a comparative golden era with 8vo's Hacienda posters, also on show at Spin's 2004 exhibition. The cultural institutions of today simply aren't as interested in commissioning designers to produce posters. "Advertising and marketing are squeezing the poster out" Brook laments. Spin knows this only too well. It produces graphic material for several London art galleries – but all too rarely is it asked to design a poster. This situation is surprising considering the place posters have occupied in the graphic heritage of museums and galleries in the past. It feels like a shamelessly missed opportunity for the reinvigoration of the poster medium that galleries are no longer actively nurturing an output of posters. Brook, however, envisages a way for posters to have a healthy future.

The Museum für Gestaltung, Zürich is one of the exceptional European examples of a museum that maintains a healthy poster commissioning policy and sells its remaining stock of exhibition posters online. Making posters available to buy is an important part of keeping the poster alive and contributes invaluably

to the museum's evolving identity. London's museums have no such policy.

Angus Hyland also points out the contrast between Britain and continental Europe in attitudes to posters and poster design, partially blaming the failing quality of British poster design on the fact that there are insufficient opportunities for designers to hone their poster-designing skills.

"I think that because they don't have the opportunity, people don't really do posters and don't do them particularly well, because, in this country, the tradition's not really there. I sound really negative but I think actually [the poster] is a dead medium here, in a sense. Or at least, it's just about hanging in there. It's a shame, for example, that theatre posters are so bad here when they could be really good.  There are occasional ones that are good but there's a low standard, and the same goes for film. If you consider, when you go to one of those shops selling antique film posters you get great ones: Get Carter; Charlie Chaplin posters – they're brilliant. But these days you get really, really poor film posters. Occasionally you see the odd independent one and you think, 'ah, that's good'. But it's really rare and there are whole outfits that do [film posters] for a living... They tend to be servicing the marketing departments rather that truly collaborating on posters, and don't have the depth of culture to bring something new to them... I think marketing and design have similar goals, they just go about them in very different ways and there is a tension – quite a good tension sometimes – between them. But sometimes its clear the power is too much in one department. I think in those whole genres where there's a low standard, like cinema, it seems that the people who produce those posters tend to be specialist and they tend to be doing it in more of a service capacity: below-the-line advertising. And they're probably taken on by those types of agencies that operate neither in high profile advertising nor graphic design.

There's this great underbelly of below-the-line advertising that hasn't got a high profile so you don't really know who's doing it – its like another world, it's the bit that's hidden away".

Much of Hyland's poster work is for cultural institutions, an area that has always been a rich source of poster design opportunities for Pentagram. Among Hyland's posters for Pentagram are those he has designed for the Crafts Council, which, he says is one of the few clients to consistently push for posters. The expense of promoting exhibitions and concerts in the legitimate poster sites in London is a contributing factor in the demise of the cultural poster. Advertising tends to price cultural posters out of the market, even in the Tube, where London Underground makes the dispensation of allowing four cultural institutions to split the space and share the cost of a regular four-sheet poster spot. Corporate-sponsored exhibitions are able to fare much better but their posters tend to be done by advertising agencies rather than graphic designers. Hyland expands on this; "Because of the effectiveness and strong tradition of the advertising industry here", he says, "it tends to have taken that space. In Europe, however, there's very clearly a difference between high and lowbrow, which is much more confused here because of the sophistication of advertising. We don't have the same tradition of patronage within the arts as in Europe. I think it's about the culture as well. We're much more of a literary race, we're good at selling things, you know, 'a nation of shopkeepers', so the culture has tended to be much more towards advertising posters as opposed to graphic posters".

There is a paradox present in the poster of today that is clearly delineated by the way it is used by the advertising industry and by graphic designers respectively. The divide also falls neatly between commercial posters (the preserve of the advertising industry) and cultural posters (the realm of graphic design). The

economic clout of the advertising industry, working on behalf of rich clients, together with the legislative commercialisation of poster sites by government means that the visual colonisation of the streets has become the preserve of the advertisers. The behemoth billboards are occupied by crass advertising that obliterate the buildings and skylines while at street level the fly-posters that alert people to events, performances, gigs and club nights are condemned as urban blight. Its no surprise that what determines your place in this hierarchy is your spending power. If you can afford the big, prominent sites you are tolerated and legalised, otherwise, you are deemed beyond control, your message is torn down and you are criminalised. The poster designer working for a small independent client has a minefield to negotiate in designing fly-posters, balancing the legal risks and costs incurred by the client and dealing with the organised gangs who actually do the midnight pasting, with getting their designs seen on the street. Henrik Kubel of London graphic design studio A2/SW/HK recounts the fly-posting hurdles in his native Denmark, where he and partner Scott Williams design posters for Aveny-T, and are often beset by the practical difficulties of fly-posting. "There's a Danish poster mafia that puts up all the posters." Kubel explains, "They're charging you and it's a whole business just putting up your posters... It's a £1.50 to put up just one poster. And horizontal posters are more expensive than vertical ones. We had posters that were put the wrong way because the client thought they'd save a bit of money".

It's a discouraging situation for both designers and clients and for talented devotees of poster design like Kubel and Williams; it's often a case of convincing the client that posters are worth commissioning. It can be a difficult task. "What the people we work for say, is that they're not selling any tickets by producing posters". Says Kubel "They sell tickets by having bus streamers, which are really commercial and rubbish,

and having cheap-looking ads. The good thing is, there's a big tradition for theatres and that sort of venue to produce posters and I've been instilling it in this client for a long time and saying we're not working for you if you're not doing posters. So his arm's twisted and he's producing, reluctantly, four posters a year".

**Post no bills: public space privatised**
Anti-fly-posting legislation also makes it difficult for even multinational companies, let alone smaller, independent or cultural institutions and companies to promote themselves with posters. Several high profile cases in the last few years have highlighted the increasingly intolerant attitude of the authorities towards fly-posting. *The Guardian* newspaper, in 2004, reported on legal action taken by Camden council against marketing executives from major record labels Sony and BMG. 'The London borough' it reported, 'today took the unprecedented step of serving anti-social behaviour orders (ASBOs) on specific executives at the two companies, which it claimed saved £8 million a year in advertising costs in Camden alone by sanctioning the illegal fly-posters. The ASBOs, usually served on unruly vandals or local troublemakers, last two years and can prevent offenders entering certain areas. The council said they were issued on the basis that fly-posting could cause 'alarm or distress.'

In September 2004, a further three ASBOs were served against staff of Diabolical Liberties, an ambient marketing company which stages promotional events and happenings as well as owning billboard sites and engaging in fly-posting. The company has an annual turnover of £10 million proof that this kind of marketing is certainly lucrative. *The Guardian* quoted Camden council's executive member for the environment as saying "This is anti-social behaviour and we don't just chase the men in the little white vans. Fly-posting has nothing to do with culture. It has everything to do with money".

It would seem that companies like Diabolical Liberties and Sony benefit financially from fly-posting in their efforts to engage with the sophisticated, media-savvy consumers who are no longer persuaded by traditional approaches to advertising. In doing so they incur the wrath of the authorities and, by drawing negative attention to their own mass-scale fly-posting, also endanger the livelihoods of small theatres, venues, independent acts and bands who rely on fly-posting as a form of affordable publicity. The Camden council executive's comments also reveal the hypocrisy at the heart of government action against fly-posting: its public relations machine tries to whip up public support for anti-fly-posting action by highlighting it as a free revenue generator for already-rich music companies. What it doesn't tell you is that fly-posting draws revenue away from advertising in the legitimate billboard and poster sites from which the government profits.

The wider London transport network is also a major source of sites for advertising posters. London Underground was once influential in the development of British graphic design under the guidance of Frank Pick, who commissioned Edward Johnson's typeface 'Railway' (still used across the network today), The iconic Underground logo and hundreds of posters by leading artists and designers. By comparison, today's London Underground is virtually bereft of notable new graphic design and is dominated by advertising posters. Prime positions on the tube and in bus shelters are hotly competed for by media agencies, that buy up the space and rent it out to advertisers. Big name, international media agencies like Clear Channel, JCDecaux and Maiden also own billboard sites – their logos discreetly marking their territory at the base of the frame. Bus shelters are also bought and sold as advertising space, with the purchaser responsible for the design and maintenance of the shelter itself as well as the posters it displays. Transport for London tenders contracts on its bus

Constantin Demner, Public Voice Boxes, recorded as part of *Walk*, Spitalfields, London 2004

Love, The Victorian Series,
posters for Fabric 2005

KerrlNoble, Bun Bun and Tony Face,
Seaside Suicide posters, 2001

shelters and takes either a flat fee or a percentage of the advertising revenue. The contracts are negotiated depending on the location, the amount the bidder is prepared to spend on, the quality and upkeep of the shelter and the amount of advertising it will give to TfL. Thus the standard of the bus shelter is likely to be in inverse proportion to the amount of money TfL makes. As with all privatisation, the concerns of profit making are at odds with the quality of experience and safety of the user. Hence the government and the media agencies land a plum deal and we get substandard bus shelters.

Thus there is a major conflict of interest about how public space should be used and regulated and the poster is at the centre of it. Fly-posting has become an alternative form of advertising for major record companies, who have used the medium to bombard the streets with posters promoting their artistes, to such an extent that it has become objectionable to local residents and authorities that see the fly-posters as vandalism and blight. Keep Britain Tidy backs the moves to prevent fly-posting categorising the poster as something ugly and dirty to be swept away. Anti-fly-posting campaigners also pillory posters, as the tools of fat-cat music industry moguls, whose profit-making posters create a massive clean-up bill which taxpayers must pick up.

So perhaps posters have become a problem because they are less beautiful than they used to be. Its true that the churn 'em out, paste 'em up mentality of the music industry means that many posters are unimaginative and uninspiring. As David Malone points out, "you very rarely see nice [posters] now... The Crafts Council ones that Pentagram did over the years have always been good, but music-wise, it used to be a regular thing, seeing fly-posters that were brilliant, but not any more. Even film posters are passé. Once one is done decently it becomes noteworthy, gets credibility and that's the thing – because

otherwise they're so boring and formulaic". The same underbelly of marketing-led design that Hyland criticises for deteriorating the film poster has also permeated the music industry. In the hands of the advertising industry the poster is treated as a cheap means to a fast buck and graphic design concerns are sidelined.

Innovative, inspiring posters are increasingly hard to come by in the world of fly-posting but some examples shine through, such as independent London design studio Love's ongoing six-year strong campaign for night club Fabric and Value and Service's recent poster campaign for photography journal *Next Level* and London duo KerrlNoble's recent work for the Crafts Council. The importance of posters to cultural clients like these is more readily recognised in Europe that Britain. Experimental Jetset works for several cultural institutions, including Amsterdam's Stedelijk Museum, which are appreciative of the poster's democratic appeal over and above targeted forms of marketing like direct marketing and emailing. "Most clients we work with are well aware that posters are less targeted", they say, "but they still find it an exciting format. They understand that it's a format that (exactly because of its history and ideological luggage) has a certain impact that can't be reached with other formats. So, we would say that the type of clients that are interested in commissioning posters are people who believe in the format of the poster itself".

Henrik Kubel of A2/SW/HK designed a series of posters to promote his seminars at Buckinghamshire College. They were seen by only a fraction of the people who might see a campaign for a new magazine or washing powder on the sides of hundreds of bus shelters but nonetheless received critical acclaim. They are typical of the migration of graphic design posters from the street to interior environments. If it weren't for the restrictive legislation on fly-posting and competition from advertising, and

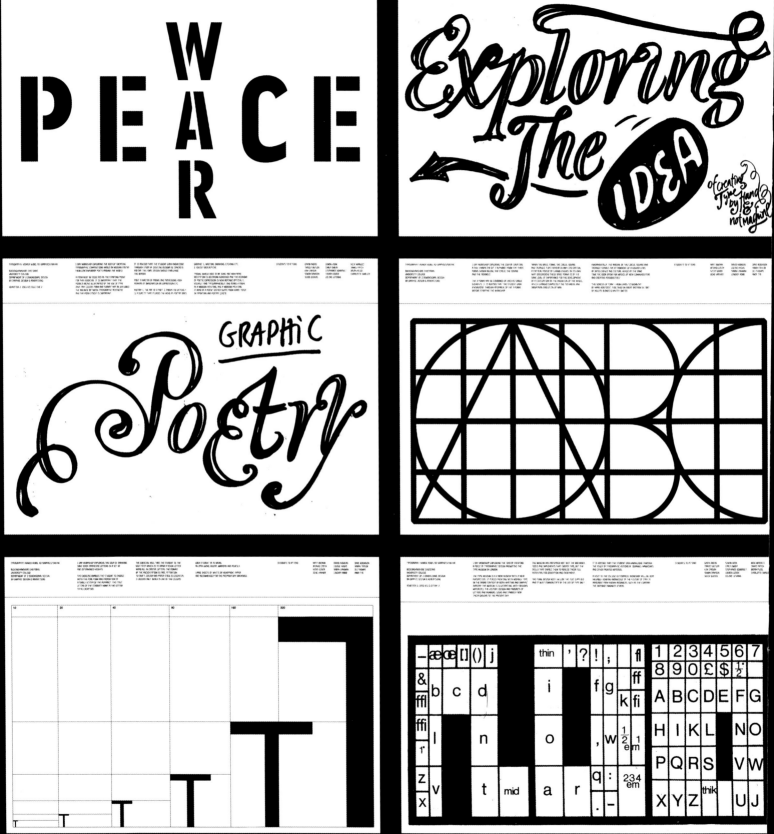

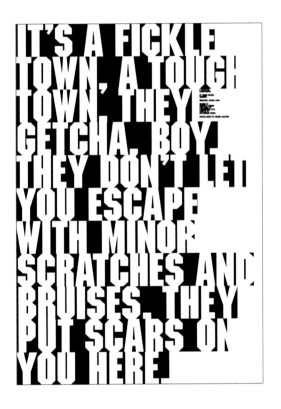

Henrik Kubel and Scott Williams, A2/SW/HK,
posters for a typographic workshop at
Buckinghamshire Chiltern University College

Jonathan Ellery / Browns, posters for
A Beautiful Catastrophe by Bruce Gilden

**PANDORA'S BOX/NYC**
**SUSAN MEISELAS**
**MAGNUM**

**PUBLISHED BY TREBRUK**
**DESIGNED BY BROWNS/LONDON**
**PRINTED BY BUTLER & TANNER**

multimedia direct marketing, many more institutions like A2/SW/HK's theatre client might see the benefits of creating a heritage through posters. Kubel carefully elaborates "To justify the posters I'm saying once your theatre's gone and all your plays have gone and you've retired or gone to a new theatre, your poster is going to be there. It's a document of what happened. If you don't produce these posters there's nothing there. There may be a review in the paper but the poster is what's seen. If you look at the poster collections in the big museums, you look at the whole French scene; you can almost see Toulouse Lautrec's life. And all those other people, although we don't know them, you can see their life through the posters and you can see the time that the poster is reflecting.

"So yes", Kubel continues, "it's a fight to get posters through and it's even a fight to get posters through that are good and that we're proud of. It's a nightmare. That's why I produced the Teaching Posters. There's still a client, so that justifies the existence of those posters, and there's a brief: it's not just me being creative and doing whatever I want to do, because I can't do that. That was one of the problems: there are a lot of posters being produced with no theme, really, and they're not really existing are they? They're just produced for the sake of producing posters. That's fine, but you need the brief, you need the thing to promote. A lot of graphic designers are producing their own posters – its one of the only aspects where you can be bold. If you've always had a passion for art and artists producing canvases and things like that... in my mind it's like producing art, it's like big icons, its large-scale icons.

Although our work is not art, it's my way of creating something, something that has a life afterwards. Something you can put on a wall and frame and actually justify the fact that its in a frame. Look at the whole history of poster design, back then they were seen as artists.

If you look at the whole of Polish design they have poster 'artists'. That was their cry for freedom and their cry for individuality and personality, that's how they were speaking – through their posters – and that was seen as art. Maybe it was seen as art because it was hard to produce them, maybe that's why, posters are still held in high esteem".

When again, today, it is hard for graphic designers to produce posters, they look for ways to keep the medium alive. London design studio Browns, self-publishes books, each one accompanied by a promotional poster. The studio's founder Jonathan Ellery also sees his poster design as a chance for self-expression and as a way of making a cultural contribution to the world. Self-promotional posters are regularly sent to other design studios and the press as well as being a point-of-sale tool for books. Ellery regularly enters posters in international poster competitions and biennales.

"To me [a poster] is more like an art piece. In a commercial world its an expression of what I can do as a designer'. Ellery says of his posters. 'I think there are those design studios out there that contribute culturally a lot more significantly than others". He continues, "The majority of design studios are based purely on cash flow and commerciality, which is fine. But those that feel a responsibility to contribute to the development of British graphic design are the ones that are doing posters".

Self-initiated posters are also vital for European designers. As well as designing posters for local events, Stockholm-based studio RBG6 creates posters to promote their own products. Such projects are a chance for experimentation and the exploration of ideas that later make it into paying jobs.

Jonathan Barnbrook
Bush Day Posters, 2003

## A Poster Democracy

At their heart posters are the most democratic form of mass communication. Anybody can create a poster whether it is with poster paint or the most sophisticated production methods. When people want to exert an opinion against the powers that be, they still do it with posters, as the anti-war/anti-Blair /anti-Bush marches all around the world in 2003 demonstrated. When graphic designers create posters there is a degree of personal involvement and personal expression involved in delivering the message because the poster exists as part of the designer's wider output and taps in to his or her ongoing obsessions, preoccupations, concerns and interests. London-based graphic designer Jonathan Barnbrook is well known for his uncompromising politicisation of graphic design. On the eve of Bush's 2004 visit to London he fly-posted the capital with anti-Blair and anti-Bush posters. Indeed the poster is at its most powerful when it is personal. The degree to which the designer is engaged with the message influences the passion with which it is relayed and the subsequent impact it has on its audience. Experimental Jetset argues that this has always been the case with posters. "We don't know if it's true that posters are becoming more personal. The whole poster culture as we know it really started with Toulouse Lautrec's posters for Moulin Rouge; very personal, expressive posters, almost autobiographical, showing his private view on public women. You can't get much more personal than that. So we think posters have always been in this state in between the public and the private. That is exactly what makes it such an interesting format. The idea of posters becoming more personal has a lot to do with the idea of designers becoming more and more 'authors'. We don't really believe that: for us, designers have always been authors".

The public power of the poster, however, is on the wane, as large-scale, crass advertising colonises the street and graphic design posters end up in interior spaces with limited audiences and graphic designers are forced to generate their own poster projects. Out on the street the poster is becoming ugly and contentious – usurped by advertising and criminalised by the authorities.

"In the US it is basically dead." Says graphic designer Stefan Sagmeister. "Posters work in societies that walk, and the only place in the US with a walking population is New York. The poster is somehow kept on artificial life support by designers and their love for it (we often design it for free or at reduced prices, just to get to do one). But even in Berlin, where I stayed for four months this year and where the poster does play a proper role, I found much street art (stencils, cut-outs, 3-D graffiti) more engaging than posters."

## Reclaiming the streets

As Sagmeister enthusiastically observes, in the wake of the poster's decline, street artists today produce the most exciting and challenging visual culture. Throughout the world, street artists are using self-initiated street interventions to reclaim the streets from the invasion of advertising and commerce. Restrictions on freedom of expression that beleaguer the poster are the call-to-arms that motivates street artists to make their mark. It is important to separate street art from graffiti in this context. Graffiti is commonly thrown in with vandalism, fly-posting and fear of crime in urban areas. The actions of street artists are not solely about public image-making or acquiring notoriety, but also about diverting attention away from the formulaic, obsequious interaction that advertising visuals demand, disrupting our conventional or habitual behaviour when traversing the street and making us think differently about the urban environment.

Typographer, designer and street artist Constantin Demner in 2004, created *Walk*, a street intervention in London that invited people living, working and

Erosie, Eroded City Cycles,
Eindhoven 2004-5

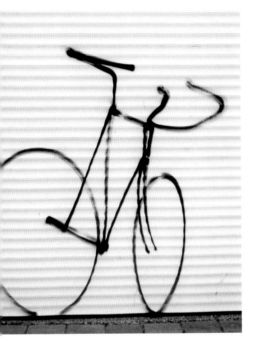

passing by in Spitalfields to divert from their ordinary routes through the district's streets and see it in a new light. *Walk* consisted of a single white-painted line, forming a winding circuit through the streets, courts and alleyways of Spitalfields, one of the most historically rich areas of London. Interrupting the line at intervals were text panels painted on the pavement, addressing the walker. Some texts beckoned the passer-by to join the walk, others imparted information and quotes about the area's history, while others still called on the walker to consider the way they interact with the street, to think of it as a living museum and an ever-evolving story.

With *Walk*, Demner wanted to test the boundaries of ownership of space that are so strongly enforced in today's city streets. The pavement, he contests, belongs to those of us who walk it, not to any authority. With *Walk* he set out to reclaim ownership of the street for the people inhabiting Spitalfields on a day-to-day basis and also to make them appreciate their surroundings by straying from their habitual paths. Demner spent months researching the history of the area and his *Walk* alerted followers to the extraordinary cultural and social diversity of Spitalfield's past. One of his text panels drew attention to a building on Brick Lane that today is a mosque. It was originally built in 1742 as a Huguenot chapel; in 1819 it was renovated and became a Methodist chapel; in 1898 it became a synagogue, finally emerging in its current incarnation as a mosque in 1976. This single building is a living monument to the layers of history that have created contemporary Spitalfields. Demner reports that the response to his work has been overwhelmingly positive. Even the policemen who stopped him on the night he painted his walk allowed him to continue once he had explained the concept behind what he was doing, and a mythology grew up about the walk locally, with residents concocting stories about who was responsible and what it was all about.

In Eindhoven, artist Erosie has created an ongoing street project called *Eroded City Cycles* that highlights the city's policy of urban regeneration. His actions take the form of stickering and spraying, focusing on the spaces in Eindhoven where freedom of movement has been restricted by so-called 'development' projects. "Some time ago," explains Erosie, "the city council of Eindhoven came up with this brilliant plan to re-do the city-centre of Eindhoven with new architecture, new public space. It was possible to do this, since there is no real 'old' city centre like in most other cities in Holland, because it got completely bombed during World War II.

The city centre of Eindhoven has always been the ugly weak spot. Unfortunately this is a good excuse to unleash prestigious architectural plans. Old charismatic buildings got destroyed to make way for new projects. Getting rid of anything in the street to attach your bike to was one of the first outcomes. It changed the city centre into a fun, shopper-friendly shopping mall. I disliked very much the arrogant attitude of forcing people in the city to use public space in one way only. For instance for a long time, a bike that was parked in the centre got 'fined' with a tag saying 'you parked your bike in an unwanted spot; please remove it'. This 'total-control' mentality gave me the idea to make a frame-sticker for bikes, and 'promote' the pirate parking of bikes in the city centre. Like turning the bike into my pirate brand, saying 'no I'm not going anywhere'! I love seeing the clusters of bikes clogging the fun-shopper flow of people. After that came the bike-throwups, as a blend between writing, drawing and pirate-bike-parking... Like putting up a bike in the street, as a reference between tagging (which is as well disliked in the street) and unwanted bikes. It's terrible to see the streets only being incorporated by ugly billboards and advertising and being completely cleaned to keep the consumers focused on consuming. Feeling safe and clean in a perfect world. Public space should be about living as well".

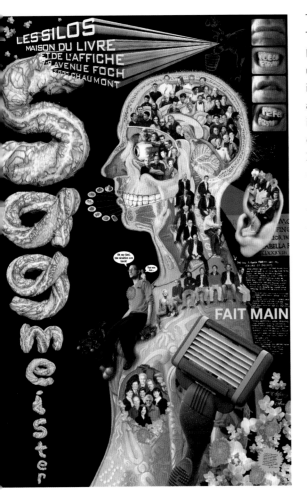

The poster is dead. Long live the poster. The poster is an endangered species. In Britain and America, especially, it is under threat. In Europe, where the poster is represented in national art collections and even has its own museum collections it's the cultural importance that is more cherished. In cities like Berlin, Paris, Zürich and Amsterdam the poster has a much healthier presence on the street. Britain, meanwhile, lacks a comprehensive centralised poster collection that is accessible to the public. The Design Museum in London has staged several retrospectives of graphic designers for whom posters were an important part of their oeuvre but there is no permanent collection. There are no doubt hundreds of small and private collections of posters hidden away in archives around Britain that could work much harder at encouraging the future of the medium if they got an airing once in a while. Many countries propagate their poster industries with festivals and biennales – the most important ones being the in Warsaw, Chaumont, Tel Aviv and Korea which celebrate international and native poster designers. If British posters were to be assured a future, then celebrating their history would be a good place to start. Such a vehicle is missing from British poster culture. Somehow, though, this is not surprising when you consider the wider political landscape and the poster's place within it. A poster culture cannot subsist on nostalgia alone but celebrating the past can help to encourage future generations and perhaps allow us to see posters worth admiring in the place they belong, on the street.

Angus Hyland insists that the future of the poster is as an art object. "I've actually created posters when there's been no need for them" he says. "And that's why they've ended up in domestic interiors and I treat them a bit like that any way. Posters should be seen as an extension of printmaking, as self-contained pieces, since there's nothing left of the graphic design poster. Although I'd be happy to do things for charities and so on, the opportunities

don't really come along because it's all sewn up by the large advertising industry that we have. They are a vanity job and should be treated like one. They have all the advantages and disadvantages of being a vanity piece – terribly indulgent but you can't expect to make an income out of it. They are in the same region as fine books – strictly for a very small audience who appreciate them. I can't see them making resurgence. Perhaps a few enlightened cultural institutions would be wise to rethink the opportunity for doing posters".

**Experimental Jetset is more optimistic:**
"It would be too easy to describe the current state of health as bad. Of course, bad design outnumbers good design, but it has always been that way. As long as there are designers who feel that design has a responsibility that goes further than only 'communicating messages to targeted audiences', and are aware that the functionality of design also has to do with its aesthetic and/or conceptual dimension, and the critical/dialectical role this dimension can play in society – as long as there are designers like that, there is hope. And, being teachers at the Gerrit Rietveld Academy, we see enough students that give us hope".

As is proved by the work of street artists like Demner and Erosie, by the dedication to the poster medium by graphic designers like A2/SW/HK, Jonathan Ellery and Experimental Jetset, and by the willingness to test the parameters of the poster medium by designers like Alon Levin, the poster still has an important role to play. What is also clear is that the poster is changing and evolving, being forced to adapt to a changing world. The poster has still has lessons to teach us – used intelligently and with imagination it still has the power to captivate us, make us alert to new things and make us question our world. From page 204 of this book are the results of an international student poster competition, which reiterate what every designer will accept: the poster is

Stefan Sagmeister, personal poster showing influences, 2004

Part of Constantin Demner's *Walk* Spitalfields, London 2004

the ultimate and most tantalising challenge. Although the traditional function of the poster – to deliver information to the masses is seriously endangered, the format still has valuable currency. Thus designers simply keep on designing them and finding new opportunities to do so. And we keep on consuming them, less as throwaway providers of information and more as art objects to be collected and treasured. The poster is dead. Long live the poster.

Angharad Lewis is a writer living in London. She writes regularly in *Grafik* magazine, where she is deputy editor and a partner in Grafik Ltd. In 2004 she curated Public Address System at the Henry Peacock Gallery in London, which brought together some of the world's most influential and innovative design talent to create specially commissioned posters. Public Address System was also exhibited at GraficEurope 2004 in Berlin. A book about the exhibition, including an essay by Angharad, is also published in 2005. Angharad has a BA in English Literature and Art History from The University of York and an MA in History of Decorative Arts and Design from the University of Brighton.

If you had a million years to do it in,
you couldn't rub out even half the
Fuck You signs in the world.
It's impossible.

**JD Salinger**
American writer
**Photograph Catherine Slessor**
London pavement 2004

Carpet all the walls with
abstractions.

**Wyndham Lewis**
British novelist, painter, critic
**Photograph Jilly Shaw**
Leicester 2004

A big hardboiled city
with no more personality than
a paper cup

**Raymond Chandler**
American writer
**Photograph Gerry Mitchell**
London 2005

BY ORDER
ATIONAL HIGHWAYS AGENCY

ALL IS A DESIGNATED
AFFITI AREA

E TAKE YOUR LITTER HOME
EC. REF. URBA 23/368

Promise large promise
is the soul of the advertisment.

**Samuel Johnson**
English poet, lexicographer, critic
**Photograph Rowan Bulmer**
Covent Garden London 1986

FIVE DIFFERENT T
-ALL IN ONE PLAC

TRADITIONAL PIZZAS · FRES
CHINESE CUISINE · STATESI
VARIETY DONUTS · EAT IN C

TAKE

JUBILEE MARKET HALL
PIAZZA · SOUTH SIDE · COV

**You look like the
second week of a garbage strike.**

**Neil Simon**
*American playwright*
**Photograph Gina Moriaty**
Hackney London 2005

Art is the only nourishment
for the starving and thirsty souls
living here on earth.

**Alphonse Mucha**
Czech poster artist
**Photograph Gina Moriaty**
London 2005

If the War had been a
battle of posters, the Germans
might have won.

**Fiona MacCarthy**
Writer on design
**Photograph Jilly Shaw**
Berlin 1998

The eyes of Doctor TJ Eckleburg
are blue and gigantic -
their retinas are one yard high.
They look out of no face, but,
instead, from a pair of
enormous yellow spectacles
which pass over a non-existent
nose. Evidently some wild
wag of an oculist set them
there to fatten his practice in
the borough of Queens, and
forgot them and moved
away. But his eyes, dimmed
a little by many paintless
days, brood on over the
solemn dumping ground.

**F Scott Fitzgerald**
American writer

*For the single brick, shall cry out from the wall* – Habakkuk (One of the Books of the Old Testament Bible)

For centuries people have written their names, initials or messages on any surface, with any coarse instrument, anywhere into the fabric of the city. "If you're going to be around all the time, you'd better put your name up" a graffiti artist said to Iain Sinclair, intrepid city walker and investigator. These abandoned public messages seem to be the city speaking to itself. The history of any city runs parallel with a history of public signs. Since time began human gestures have clearly communicated a variety of emotions, directions, qualitative judgements and so on. It's impossible to legislate against public gestures because we have created a universal language of approval and disapproval, contempt and superstition (like spitting on the ground to bring us luck). With the need to communicate over distance and to many, public signs have taken many forms and still concern City Governors.

By the 18th century, every trade and shop in London had its own painted sign. The Society of Sign Painters exhibited its products, the pedestrian had to 'read the street' and the designers of signs had to be exact and competitive. Signs and plaques were carved into the stone of some buildings; even coal hole covers were decorated. When stone was introduced into the city to replace cobbles, pavement artists, with cheap chalks could reproduce 'art' with garish colour and the common message 'All my own work.' The city was and is a labyrinth of signs and private and official marks. There had always been handbills wrapped around the posts of the street, but with the advent of the 'wondrously pictorial', trades were denoted by large papier-mâché symbols of boots, fish, cigars, kettles and so on, suspended over doorways.

Advertising changed 'street-art's' form. The 19th century saw the innovation of the advertising hoarding and the enlarged images became appropriate to the city itself – big, gaudy, colourful and ever-changing. The walls of the city became a permanent display of forthcoming, recent and old sensations. The sandwich man appeared in the 1830s, then the advertisement drawn by horses, then the electric advertisement. Soon advertising was everywhere – above ground, underground and in the heavens. Aldous Huxley in *Brave New World* writes that 'the electric sky-signs effectively shut off the outer darkness.'

Various London borough councils fear that our streets are now blighted, property prices are falling because of the tatty nature of the urban fabric; the councillors want to get the cleansing department unleashed. I can see their point, but cities have always been places of civic demonstration, public spaces have always been built into them.

Early in Renaissance Florence, paintings of criminals or the arrested were hung outside the Bargello, the prison and execution place, and left to fade and blister. Like the 'Wanted' posters of today. Graffiti can be seen in the excavations of the ancient Pompeii. It is the easiest way for an individual to make their views (on literally anything) known to the general public. Spray-cans, chalk, carving tools, pasted-up messages, cheap paper stencils – the tools are commonplace, the canvas vast. 'Kilroy wos ere'. Three-dimensional signs outside shops have now been superseded by neon and plastic and grotesque, revolting typography. The rich imagery of the traditional pub sign continues but the beauty and symbolism of the barber's stripped pole, the pawnbroker's sign and the cigar store identity, for example, have almost completely disappeared.

The public poster receives only token interest now, because our city life has become saturated with signs, symbols, offers, proclamations, exhortations and promises of a better here and now.

Amongst and against all this competing graphic junk, the professional designer has not only to operate but also to try to make memorable images that maybe can 'stop the traffic.'

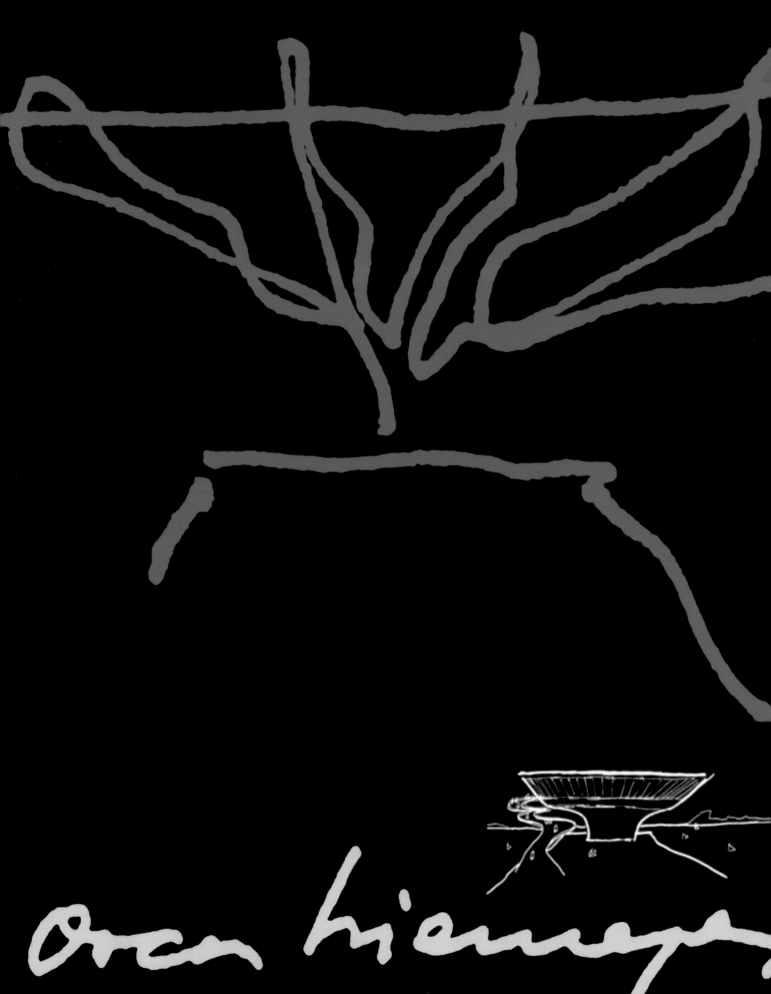

Oscar Niemeyer
Royal Gold Medallist 1998

Gallery One
October 6-31 1998

RIBA Architecture Centre
Royal Institute of British Architects
66 Portland Place
London W1N 4AD
Telephone 0171 307 3699

Opening times
Monday, Wednesday, Friday and Saturday
08 00-18 00
Tuesday and Thursday
08 00-21 00
Admission free

I was trained in a very rigorous school. My first job was in an advertising agency that for me and for the people who paid me, was a disaster. This has clouded my appreciation of persuasive advertising ever since. My teachers in later employment like Geoff White, Hans Schleger, Bill Slack, all developed and refined the early lessons taught at The London School of Printing by Tom Eckersley, Derek Birdsall and Ian Bradbury. My freelance experience with Bob Gill and D&AD and later in Canada, New York and the UK simply enriched a design approach that started in 1957. Cities change, design is subject to trends and fashions, our industry has changed beyond recognition, but 40 years later my graphic sensibilities and affiliations have remained constant. I believe in 'modern movement' typography, and the 'rules' of dynamic proportion, I believe in the 'musicality' of layout and the surprise of the eccentric.

My heroes are Hans Schleger, who taught me to edit a line of type with such refinement that the result is beyond criticism and the painter Sam Francis who showed me how to place work in a format beautifully, without using some Corbusian grid. And Bob Gill because everything he does 'stops the traffic'. Graphic designers are best when they are anonymous (AM Cassandre said this about poster work), they are at their best when they are true to their own design philosophy, and speak openly to clients, printers and all other associates. Our industry is to do with interdependence and can only be successful if all the skills and talents of the numerous trades involved can be harmoniously brought together. "Leave your egos at the door" Quincy Jones said on one famous occasion – this applies everyday in our work.

By May 1991 I had left two years employment, as assistant designer and art editor on *The Architectural Review*. I decided to work from home. At a public relations event at the Imagination

offices on Store Street, I met Dennis Sharp again. We had worked closely and well together on 'Space and Performance', June 1989 (*The Architectural Review*, AR 1108 – Dennis was guest editor for this special theatre issue) and he invited me to design the promotion and catalogue for the forthcoming Santiago Calatrava retrospective to be held at RIBA in the autumn of 1992.

Calatrava was born in 1951 at Benimamet, Valencia, and studied architecture in Valencia and engineering in Zürich. At 30, his first practice was established in Zürich and eight years later the Paris office opened. Before RIBA he had exhibited sculptures in Zürich, architecture in Toronto; drawings in Los Angeles; with travelling exhibitions in the USA and Canada. Lotus Documents, Birkhauser, Croquis and Artemis Verlag by 1992 had all published books on his work. Since the early Valencia years his work has been rewarded, with honours from the cities of Berlin, Paris, Barcelona and Zürich. At the time of the London exhibition Calatrava was to receive The Gold Medal from the Institution of Structural Engineers. James Sutherland the British engineer called him 'a one man orchestra'. As a youngish architect he had designed and built wonderful bridges, bus shelters, community centres, libraries, pavilions; a Swiss theatre and television studio; a Canadian galleria. His most publicised project was the Stadelhofen Railway Station in Zürich. Calatrava's work increased in size and prestige, and in the early 1990s he opened a Valencia office

The photograph for our poster was made by the American photographer John E. Linden and shows a detail of the Alamillo Bridge in Seville, shot at midnight. The extra colours and the type arrangement just happened effortlessly. Dennis and I made a symbol for the show, the catalogue, which sold out and went into a second edition, various invitations and exhibition tokens. Dennis

Sharp Architects curated and designed the show, which was a huge success.

As a kind of by-product to the main event we also produced two instant posters for a Calatrava lecture 'Architecture and the Dynamics of Structure' for 20 October at RIBA. And for the following day Felix Candela's lecture 'A lifetime in concrete' at the same location. Both poster designs used the same printer, identical colours and black and white photography and although the content and layout is very different a kind of family resemblance happened.

Two years later, as part of the Spanish Arts Festival, Calatrava exhibited new projects at The Bruton Street Gallery in Mayfair. Dennis Sharp Architects designed the show 'Recent Projects'. The illustration, bleached-out, is of The Trinity Bridge, Salford and was printed with a wonderful solid depth of colour, by Newnorth of Bedford.

In 1996 the same team was invited by Wates City Properties plc to present Calatrava's design proposals for the renewal of Brittanic Tower in the City of London. The former headquarters of British Petroleum was to be turned into new office space, the tower renovated and extended with shops and restaurants at street level, and a stunning restaurant at the very top. With endless planning and political difficulties the scheme was rejected and London was denied a new, unique architectural symbol years before the advent of Foster's Swiss Reinsurance Tower.

A further outcome from all the Calatrava work was that we became friends with one of his photographers, Paolo Rosselli. Dennis Sharp, in the pedestrianised Woburn Walk WC1, ran a bookshop with a small gallery attached 'The Volume Gallery', and we presented Paolo's very first London exhibition in 2000.

Paolo Rosselli was born in Milan in 1952. He studied architecture but after obtaining his degree, decided to work

Collage: Lucien Kroll
Poster: Malcolm Frost | Igma
© Book Art 2002

# Spontaneous Cities & Gardens

Private View:
Tuesday 29 October 2002
18.30 - 20.30 hours
RSVP

Exhibition:
30 October - 23 November 2002
Monday - Friday
11.00 - 18.00 hours

The VOLUME Gallery
Book Art & Architecture Bookshop
12 Woburn Walk
Bloomsbury
London WC1H OJL
telephone 020 7387 5006
fax 01707 875286
email sharpd@globalnet.co.uk

Simone & Lucien

# Kroll

exclusively as a photographer. He has just published a book on the work of Giuseppe Terragni with Skira. He is the author of a dozen books and has exhibited in the USA and in most European countries. He has been associated with Santiago Calatrava for many years. The photograph we used in the poster is of Calatrava's Airport Railway Station at Lyon. For me, the exceptional long-focused vision of Paolo Rosselli makes his work unique as an architectural photographer. He manages to retain the precision and timelessness of the early photographic pioneers with an innate sense of the harmonics of now. I love working with his images, because as a designer you soon realise you don't have to strain too hard graphically to make something very powerful.

Felix Candela was born in Madrid in 1910, and studied architecture there. From 1939 he lived and worked in Mexico and in 1947 became a Mexican citizen. He achieved beauty of form through his amazing understanding of materials and their use under stress – he translated scientific engineering into art.

Candela said that 'he cut himself loose from all conventional methods of calculation'. In the 1970s he left Mexico to live in the USA; he died in 1994. He left to art, engineering and architecture the most remarkable structures – revolutionary, poetic, and the massively substantial with the attributes of sensuous nature. He wrote that 'theory must be accompanied by progressive realisation – creativity must combine structural intuition with the visual rightness of design.'

Imre Makovecz's buildings give the impression of coming alive. He always stood outside the architecture produced by the official Hungarian State Building Department, which is largely described as soul-less, Soviet-style or anonymous. Makovecz uses traditional organic Hungarian architecture as a starting point of his work now, that resists conformity, and tries to re-identify a local tradition.

Dennis Sharp and myself were asked by RIBA to design the poster shown here and a cheap flyer to promote the Makovecz exhibition. But, even with the support of the Prince of Wales, his school, and the RIBA, the show was canned.

In 1998 Oscar Niemeyer was awarded The Gold Medal, by the RIBA, for outstanding architectural achievement. Dennis Sharp Architects designed a small exhibition and we made the publicity. The A2 poster was silk-screened by G&B Arts, London, in three colours with the background made up of a percentage of red under the blue.

Kisho Kurokawa's world exhibition came to London from its starting point in Paris. From London it travelled to Chicago, then to Amsterdam and Berlin finishing in Tokyo, two years later. Dennis Sharp Architects designed the huge show at RIBA and we designed the publicity and the catalogue. Kurokawa was born in Nagoya City and graduated from Kyoto University; he established Kisho Kurokawa & Associates in Tokyo in 1964. For RIBA we produced an exhibition symbol, invitations, ads, a guide and souvenirs. In the next few years we also made publicity and catalogues for Kurokawa shows at The Cube Gallery, Manchester and at Kew Gardens. His best-known photographer, Tomio Ohashi, also exhibited prints at Volume Gallery to great acclaim.

The Belgium architect Lucien Kroll and his wife Simone produced a show at The Volume Gallery, London in the autumn of 2002. We made the poster. The exhibit was one, huge, floor-to-ceiling piece of photographic paper with images and the storyline printed on the single surface. The poster was a segment of the show with the specific details scattered around. My colleague Graeme Martin (who owns the production house, Igma) and I splashed into his wonderful computer system and extracted this final piece. The brilliance of the computer is that a thousand design and layout possibilities can be

available in a second, with always the proviso that the direction is talked through (spoken about) first. Our image was so seductive that the poster was recommended as a 'Delight' page for *The Architectural Review*.

The Michael Wilford lecture, at The Building Centre, was just a part of an exhibition about one building – The Lowry Centre in Salford, Manchester. The idea of an exhibition featuring one building with an opportunity to hear the actual architect speak about the work is hugely appealing, and as Michael Wilford is a terrific communicator, the event was a sell-out.

The poster for Paolo Soleri, was made to publicise a forthcoming book, published by Arizona State University, written by the late Jeffery Cook and edited by Dennis Sharp. It shows a wall detail and long view of part of the Cosanti Foundation work. Soleri was born in Turin in 1919, studied at the Polytechnic School of Architecture, left for America and was apprenticed to Frank Lloyd Wright in 1947. He returned to Italy for just two years and in 1955 made a permanent home in the USA.

Modernism's transformations, the poster for Tony Fretton's DoCoMoMo lecture, October 2003, shows the clarity of Adrian Frutiger's Univers masterpiece.

The Gateshead-Sage poster announced an exhibition of Norman Foster's work and advertised a list of talks associated with various aspects of the building. The photograph is by Nigel Young. All three posters were designed for The Building Centre Trust for events in their gallery spaces in Central London.

Manfredi Nicoletti, the most talented draftsman I've ever known, had a show at The Volume Gallery and we made the simple black poster. Dennis Sharp had an anniversary exhibition at RIBA and we made four posters illustrating his many formidable talents, two of which are shown later.

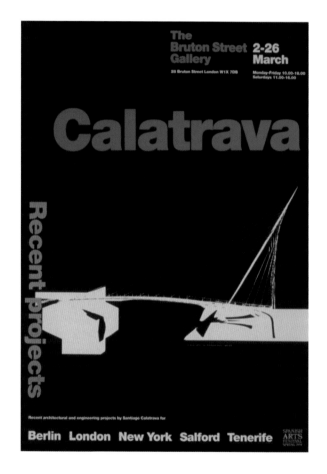

**Calatrava Santiago**

Santiago Calatrava's art brings an invigorating breath of life into the confused and disorientated architectural panorama of the present day. *Fons Carolina*

**City Point**
A new Tower for
The City

An exhibition of
design proposals for
the renewal of
Britannic Tower

November 28 until
December 20 1996
Daily 09.00 – 18.00hrs.
Admission free

Britannic Tower
Ropemaker Street
London EC2
Ground floor gallery

WATES CITY

© Bookart 1992

**Santiago Calatrava**

**RIBA Lecture**

**"Architecture and the dynamics of structure"**

**20.10.1992 18.15**

Lecture sponsored by the British Cement Association
and supported by British Airways

Tickets: RIBA members £4.00
Students £2.50 Non-members £5.50
Credit card bookings 071 251 0791

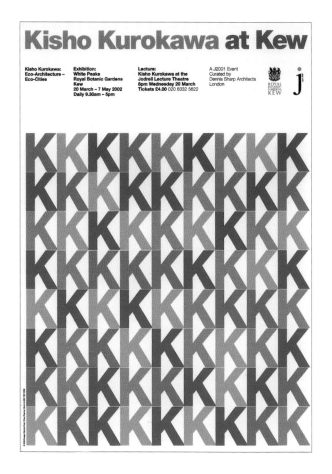

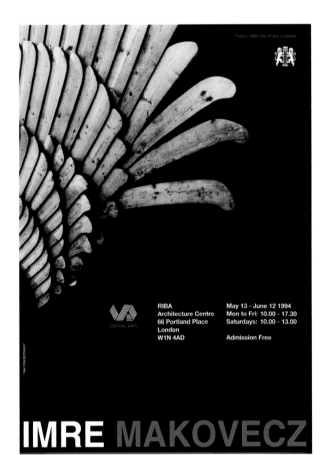

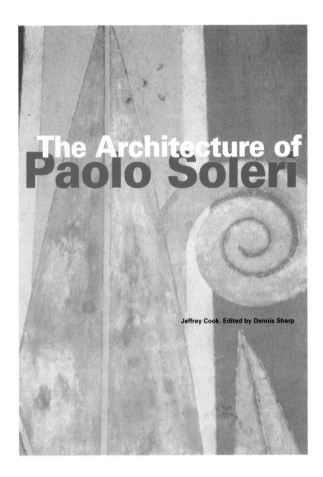

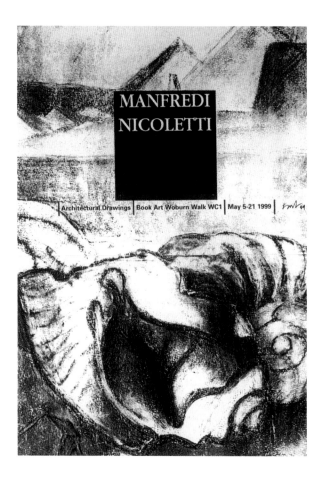

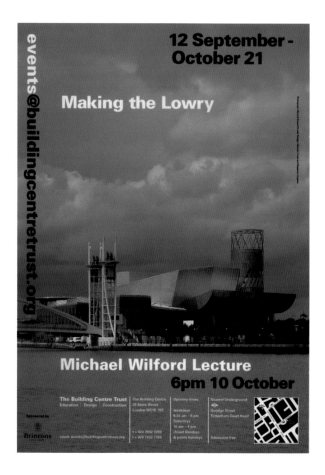

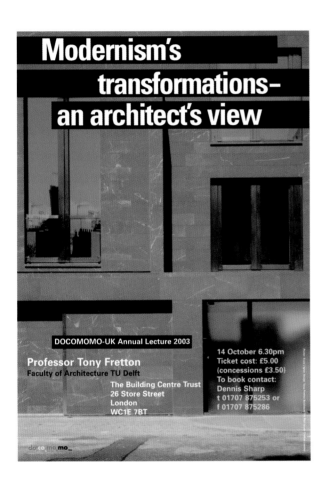

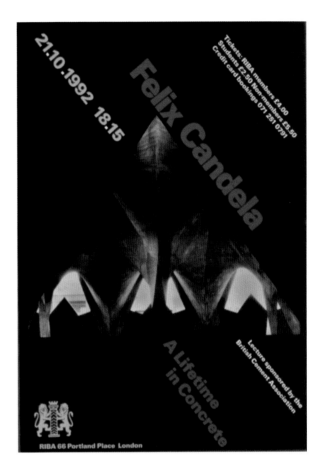

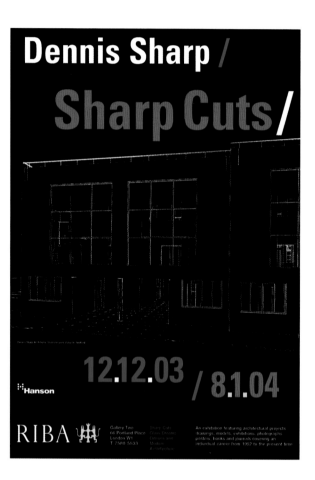

**The Sage Gateshead**

**The Sage Gateshead**
Music and Light
Foster and Partners
An exhibition at
The Building Centre
Store St London WC1

Wednesday 9 February -
Saturday 12 March 2005

**FIGUERAS**
INTERNATIONAL SEATING

thrislington cubicles

**waagner biro**

This exhibition forms part of the
Products in Practice series which
explores the way design & materials
work together through architecture.

Opening Lecture by
Spencer de Grey, Deputy Chairman,
Foster and Partners -
Tuesday 8 February 6:30pm

Kate Maestri, Proto Studio and
Dane Architectural Solutions -
Monday 28 February 6:30pm

Further lectures in the series:
Johann Sischka
of Waagner Biro steel fabricators -
Monday 21 February 6:30pm

Jason Flanagan, Partner,
Foster and Partners and
Ian Knowles of Arup Acoustics -
Tuesday 8 March 6:30pm

To book a place on any of the lectures:
E: events@buildingcentretrust.org
T: 020 7692 6208
www.buildingcentretrust.org

**The Building Centre Trust**
education | design | construction

Photography: Nigel Young / Foster and Partners   Poster design: Frost | Igma 2005

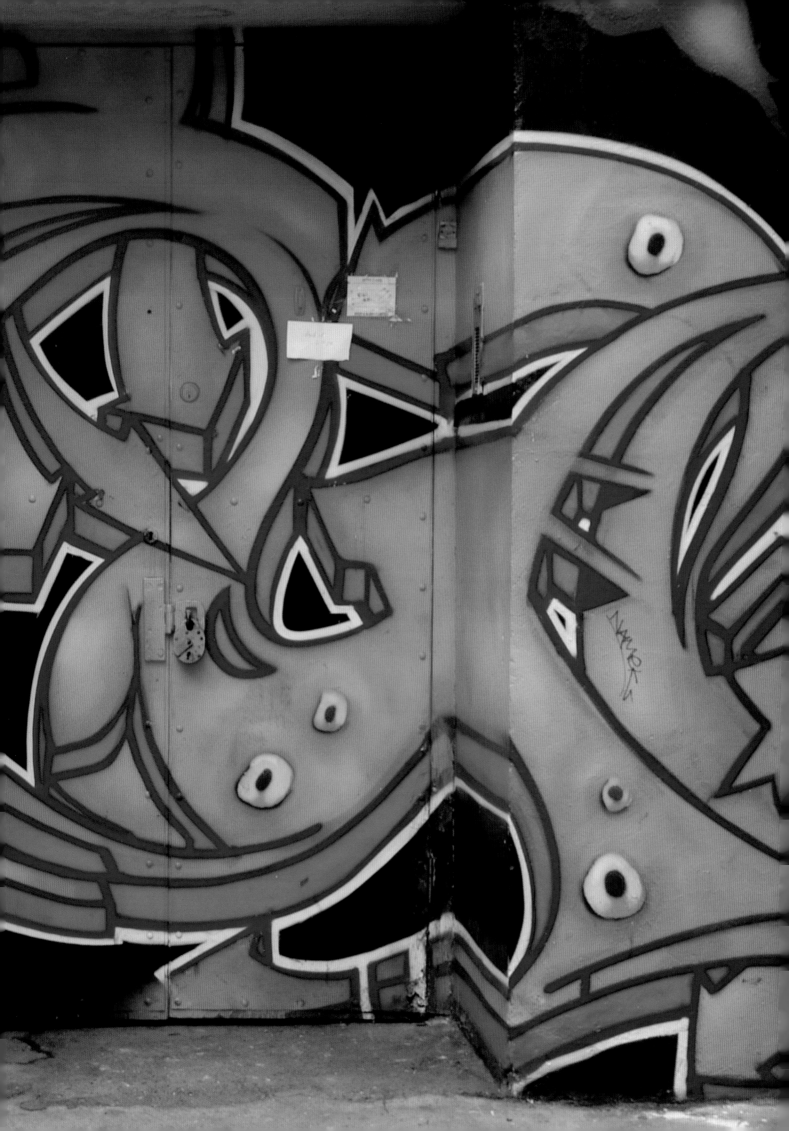

The
National Ballet
of Canada
Kraanerg
Nov 18-22
O Keefe Centre

In *The Temptation of Dr Antonio*, a billboard (featuring Anita Ekberg) comes alive and the good doctor's fantasy becomes reality. This was Frederico Fellini's contribution to four filmed stories that were inspired by Boccaccio. *Hello Boys'* (featuring Eva Herzigova) stopped the traffic everywhere, raised onanism to levels of an Olympic event, and launched a thousand soft-porn magazines. As *The Guardian* newspaper so poignantly put it (in 1968) 'so he's seen your bra ad, but will he buy one?' Sex sells everything. So all the account executives say.

This idea started many moons ago, before the turn of the 20th century. Jules Cheret's pin-up girl poster style in the 1890s idealised the cheerful, smiling, youthful, colourful girl that was asked to sell everything. From shoes, medicine, ice-rinks, revues, the Folies to cocoa, newspapers and petrol. In the spirit of the fin de siecle, Jules Cheret made over a 1000 posters, and was called 'the inventor of the gallery on the street'.

The public poster has now really become a dichotomy in all our daily lives. Here displayed for all to see is a large sheet of printed paper, that can persuade us that the new Fiat is indispensable for our lives; mobilise us to war; stimulate us to join a yoga evening class; expound; provoke; inform us about future entertainment and dire consequences. We may not notice (or even be curious about) any of this at all. But we can be assured that within days these old provocations will have gone, and new sets of pasted-up messages have appeared. The designers of these 'momentary' sheets go to extraordinary lengths to make the public take note. And even though there many be thousands of copies printed and placed in strategic locations – the finger-crossed hope is that the curious will turn into buyers. Persuasive posters go unnoticed often, because their everyday environment is filled with commonplace activity and human distraction.

Many posters are so badly designed that no one sees them anyway. Quite often poster sites are clogged with competing messages and ideas, so that the whole area becomes like a thick graphic fog. The public poster is transient – it has to live in the moment.

Surprisingly from Manet, Bonnard and Lautrec in the late 1800s to Hockney and Rauschenberg now, painters find the medium extremely appealing. We can academically investigate, deconstruct, x-ray the great paintings of the past (Giorgione's *La Tempesta* is still, 500 years after it was made, being forensically argued about) but we never discuss the effectiveness of a Leger, or Kollwitz poster. Most artists' posters fail as pieces of 'public art' because they don't have any adequate knowledge of typography (why should they?). Their completed works have little logic, dynamic rhythm or contrast – the whole sheet tends to be filled with a kind of all over illustrative sameness. The graphic designer, on the other hand, knows by instinct, education or experience that the poster is the sum of all its many different details. The words must be legible (taken in quickly); the image must have a dynamic (must be 'read' and must lead somewhere); the colour must evoke a strong response; in a competitive environment the poster (the message) must remain in the memory. Finally (the tricky part) the poster must contribute, environmentally, to a common aesthetic sense and artistic awareness.

Performing arts companies or associations commissioned all the examples shown next. The posters function was to sell theatre tickets (get bums onto seats) for live performances of ballet, opera, drama, classical music and jazz. For the designer the subject of this type of work is already rich in illustrative content (the history of past performances and so on) the photographers and/or illustrators that are drawn to this work are usually creatively excellent.

Most productions are generally, or

fleetingly known: *Giselle, Marriage of Figaro* etc, and the poster only has to re-establish a memory (usually a fond one). The poster, in this case, must express the essential quality of live performance, namely the risk-taking and adventure.

The problems we personally discovered when working in this field were bizarre and unquantifiable. Nick Milton and I first worked for The National Ballet of Canada in 1970. The Ballet, under the direction of Celia Franca, produced a Bejart-choreographed work, called *Kraanerg*, with an electronic score and op-art sets by Vasarely. We made the poster. A 'posterised' black rehearsal photograph was printed on a silver ground. The actual ballet was so extreme, Toronto critics said 'stay away'; our posters, unexpectedly, found their way inside Toronto cheapo giftshops, sold as pieces of 1960's psychedelia.

We were then asked to work for The National Opera as well. The Opera had previously used painters to draw their posters, with little communication success. Our poster for *Die Fledermaus* and *Rigoletto* – a graphic soundwave, was removed from the site walls and found later, framed in people's homes. Louis Quillico (a Rigoletto of genius) sold the production out, although his name didn't appear on the poster.

*Giselle* shows Victoria Tennett (a principal dancer) leaping over the type. For *The Nutcracker* we photographed our partner's daughter, Roshanna, surrounded by cartoon-like figures (by Pen Inc – a Toronto studio of illustrators). Neither poster tried to specifically describe the production, but simply communicated a sense of expectation. None of the design partners had seen or heard *The Marriage of Figaro* but we ordered the elaborate cake, shot it and added the funny type. The client was delighted with all of the outcomes. Because of the exposure the design group was now being regarded as 'expert' in graphic cultural matters. We started working for The National Arts Centre in Ottawa.

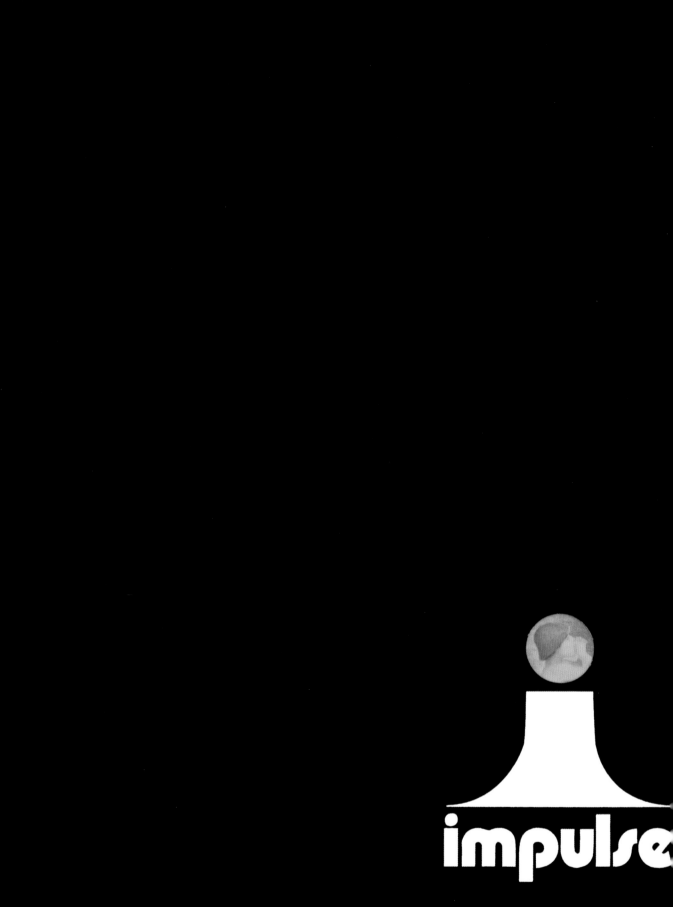

*Mrs Warren's Profession* uses an actual Victorian photograph of a well-known prostitute, and the type is a parody of a calling card. *Oh, What a Lovely War* shows the actual Canadian version of the Kitchener poster and the typography is supposed to be jolly, musical and Lubalinesque. From GBS at The NAC we were invited to work for the Shaw Festival, based at Niagara-on-the-Lake in Ontario. The resulting introductory poster – with the N symbol – proves that simple black-and-white printing can be both powerful, and evoke many associations.

In the 1980s I ran a small studio in Covent Garden, Central London, and we made three posters for The British Council's music department. The City of London Sinfonia had 12 string-players and we graphically described this by silhouetting the number and type of instruments involved. The Council toured the Clarke Tracey Quintet and Joanna MacGregor overseas, and the spaces left at the bottom of the posters were for various overprinting. I realised that to bleed the colour (MacGregor) was a better solution than leaving a white strip, because the quality, or design, of the overprinting didn't matter as the poster retained its integrity. Interestingly the Clarke Tracey poster was printed in both silk-screen and litho techniques together.

The National Ballet poster was for touring companies and specific details were silk-screened into any space

From a designer's point of view to produce this type of work is completely satisfactory. To be involved with the performing arts is stimulating and the final posters, in this particular case, will provide the designer (or the studio) precious public relations mileage.

(The designer that created the identity for The National Theatre – then at The Old Vic, before the move to The South Bank – actually made his posters, advertising, programmes, cast-lists, an integral and enhancing part of the whole

theatre experience. Ken Briggs made all this work and it is still regarded as the epitome of graphic design brilliance).

There is a huge industry recording, branding, marketing and selling recorded music, most of it careless of any extraordinary sound quality. But a certain enthusiastic minority requires and demands sound reproduction that is akin to actual performance. In the summer of 1974, we started working for Impulse Loudspeakers. Impulse sold a very expensive product that claimed, through their systems one could hear David Oistrakh's violin strings sweating. For the 'Rolls Royce' of loudspeakers we wanted to design publicity that had 'natural' connections with sophistication, refinement and a range of 'colours'. Our first publicity shoot was in Lord Leighton's house (now a museum) in West London – using his 'orientalist' decor as a backdrop. For the second series we emphasised the names and images of ancient instruments (Ta'us, Kora and Lali) and photographed at the Horniman Museum, Dulwich. The poster, shown here, uses a detail from the Georges Seurat painting *Une Baignade* with the young bather shouting, incorporated into the company logo.

On December 13, the feast day of St Lucy, the youngest daughters of Christian families in Sweden wear crowns with lit candles, serve coffee, cakes and sing special celebratory songs. (Before the calendar was reformed this feast day fell on the shortest day of the year). Lucy (or Lucia) was martyred in the fourth century at Syracuse, Sicily (Caravaggio painted *The Burial of St Lucy* there in 1608 – after his prison escape from Malta), her name means 'light' and she has become the patron saint of festivals.

Design Workshop, by 1973, had opened a second office in Ottawa, simply because of the volume of our Federal Government work. One of our most prestigious projects, at this time, was

the design of the symbol and all related promotion for the celebration of Canada's National Day. The poster shows the radiating symbol bursting over the Ottawa Parliament Building.

The poster 'Coast to Coast' uses a Pollock theatre device was used because the advertised plays covered a long history, style and content and we felt we needed some general, brightly evocative image.

The Harrogate Arts Festival has been established for years. Although it is not as internationally famous as, say, the Edinburgh Festival, it is significant events locally and beyond. When I was with Hans Schleger (1976) we designed the new identity for The Edinburgh Festival, since changed (many times) – and the experience was unforgettable.

For Harrogate (see page 118) we used a double take on Eadweard Muybridge.

When they happen Film Festivals are always front-page news. Venice, Cannes, London and Berlin are hugely important commercial and artistic events for the industry. (See page 136)

Festivals are usually a time given over to a group-spiritedness, and a time when we forget differences and hope we carry forward new friendships and our capability for diverse creativity. Next time you light a candle (in any circumstance), give St Lucy a second thought.

National Ballet of Canada
O'Keefe Centre

Giselle. April 16 to 19.
Swan Lake, Concerto Barocco,
The Lesson, Phases,
Solitaire. April 21 to 25.

# Giselle

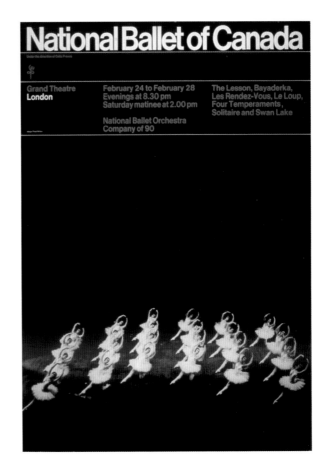

# National Ballet of Canada

Under the direction of Celia Franca

Grand Theatre
**London**

February 24 to February 28
Evenings at 8.30 pm
Saturday matinee at 2.00 pm

National Ballet Orchestra
Company of 90

The Lesson, Bayaderka,
Les Rendez-Vous, Le Loup,
Four Temperaments,
Solitaire and Swan Lake

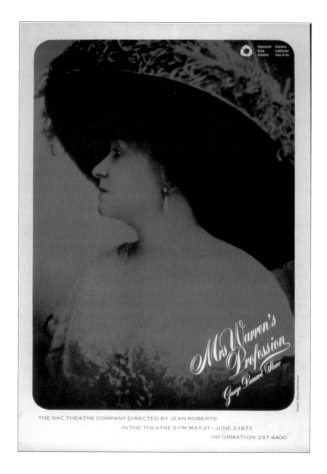

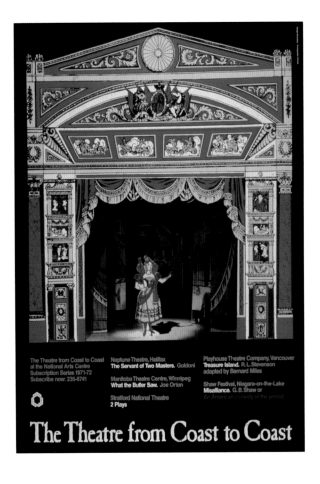

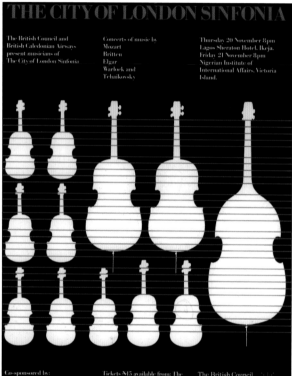

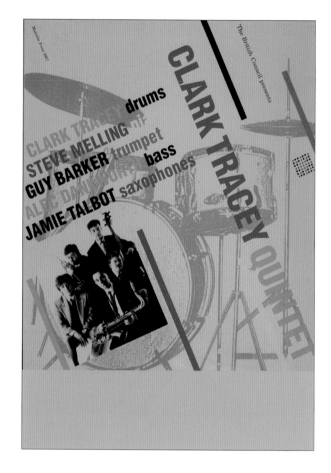

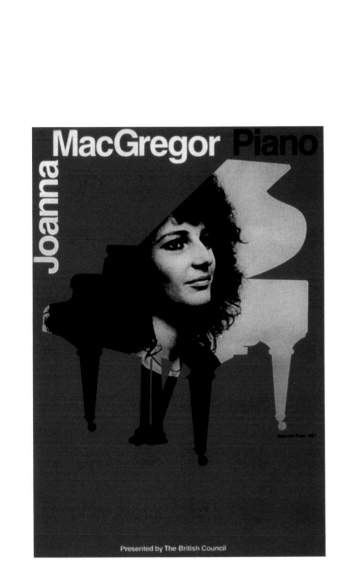

CiRCUS CiRCUS
WITH NORMAN BARRETT: THE WORLD'S GREATEST RINGMASTER

BLACKHEATH SE3
A2 SHOOTERS HILL ROAD · SUPER EASTER CIRCUS!

FROM 23 MAR UNTIL 5 APR

DIAL A SEAT: 0871 210 2100

ZIPPOS ZIPPOS

The Link The Link

SKI WEAR SALE
1000 NIKE SHOES
£35 or ess!!

THIS WAY TO
SUBWAY
The world's favourite sandwich

EuroNation *Phonecard
The best phonecard to call East & West Europe

talk2U
in...EUROPE & USA

More Than
8 Hours on £5

Austria      Germany     Norway
Belgium     Italy        Sweden
Canada      Ireland      Switzerland
Denmark     Luxembourg   UK
France       Netherlands  USA

More Than 6 Hours on £5
Australia          New Zealand

Australia
Canada          £5 min
Czech Rep.      8 Hrs
France           Local Access 0207
Germany         £5 min
New Zealand
Poland           4 Hrs
Russia           Free Access 0800
USA

PLUS
"FREESTYLE"
FREE CALLS TO THE ABOVE DESTINATIONS BETWEEN
8PM AND 9PM EVERY FRIDAY NIGHT !!!

Fishcotheque
Open
Fresh Fish · Pies (Pukka)
Fried & Grilled Chicken
Burgers · Omelettes

All our fish is freshly
prepared in our shop.

STANDARD
PLACE

NO BUSES TO BE PARKED ON THE ROAD

WILLS'S CIGARETTES — S. BLACK (PLYMOUTH ARGYLE)
WILLS'S CIGARETTES — J. CONNOR (SUNDERLAND)
WILLS'S CIGARETTES — D. J. ASTLEY (ASTON VILLA)
WILLS'S CIGARETTES — J. COULTER (EVERTON)
WILLS'S CIGARETTES — S. MATTHEWS (STOKE CITY)
WILLS'S CIGARETTES — E. J. SUGGETT (BRADFORD)

WILLS'S CIGARETTES — J. McMENEMY (MOTHERWELL)
WILLS'S CIGARETTES — R. STARLING (SHEFFIELD WEDNESDAY)
WILLS'S CIGARETTES — J. McILWANE (SOUTHAMPTON)
WILLS'S CIGARETTES — J. MORTON (WEST HAM UNITED)
WILLS'S CIGARETTES — W. MILLS (ABERDEEN)
WILLS'S CIGARETTES — J. PICKERING (SHEFFIELD UNITED)

WILLS'S CIGARETTES — W. MILLERSHIP (SHEFFIELD WEDNESDAY)
WILLS'S CIGARETTES — J. HOLLIDAY (BRENTFORD)
WILLS'S CIGARETTES — S. WEAVER (NEWCASTLE UNITED)
WILLS'S CIGARETTES — E. J. VINALL (NORWICH CITY)
WILLS'S CIGARETTES — E. V. WRIGHT (LIVERPOOL)
WILLS'S CIGARETTES — T. WALKER (HEART OF MIDLOTHIAN)

WILLS'S CIGARETTES — E. SANDFORD (WEST BROMWICH ALBION)
WILLS'S CIGARETTES — R. STUART (MIDDLESBROUGH)
WILLS'S CIGARETTES — F. WORRALL (PORTSMOUTH)
WILLS'S CIGARETTES — H. CARTER (SUNDERLAND)
WILLS'S CIGARETTES — A. F. LYTHGOE (HUDDERSFIELD TOWN)
WILLS'S CIGARETTES — W. FURNESS (LEEDS UNITED)

# Football Heaven
## Visions of the Beautiful Game

The poster 'Western Art' features John Hoyland, a painter frequently collected by The British Council and the Titian is just a personal favourite of mine. Perhaps over 20 years later some other image would be used to represent 'now' in the Western Art poster? But the most interesting and magical thing, for me personally, is that graphic design has the speed to present great concepts in an instant. Titian-Hoyland, the Renaissance-Now, two images and four words and 500 years of art can be imagined by all of us. The image from the movie *2001* of the transference between primeval hammering ape to space travel, took seconds and knocks everyone out, but in print we do this constantly. It's almost a prerequisite of a graphic designer to try to understand the most complicated things – mechanical or philosophical. We are never present to talk people through a piece of work, to explain, to demonstrate or to teach – in order to communicate we must understand as a layman.

The Josephine Baker House was an exhibition at Henry Peacock Gallery featuring Dan Brady's design for a fantasy apartment in *Unite d'Habitation*, to be shared by the entertainer and the architect. Baker and Le Corbusier had an unlikely affair – very brief – in 1929. The old blue Baker image shown, suggests a retirement 'home' apartment was being exhibited. The Corbusier-type stencil lettering is iconic and the round framed glasses a symbolic Corb giveaway.

*Football Heaven* was made to attract financial and/or editorial support for a book about the Arts associated with the beautiful game. There were sections in the book on architecture, literature, photography, graphics and so on – the poster was to gather interest for the enterprise. The old cigarette cards are specific and dated but the regimentation of the layout makes a stunning visual. We are still waiting at this time for a response about sponsorship or help. The project has become one of those bottom-drawer jobs.

"Excuse me, can you spare a moment? Could you take a picture of me and the wife and kids?"

Anyone and everyone can use a camera. Cameras are now left, as instant-visual-memento-recorders, in our hotel rooms, along with the key to the mini-bar and the welcoming basket of freebies. You can buy a pre-loaded camera at a stationery store, take 24 frames and have the whole roll printed (4x5 colour prints) in an hour for less than $10. George Eastman had made this arrangement available over a hundred years before. "You click the shutter we'll do the rest".

Photography has always been seen as an invention, yet its aesthetic references have always followed Fine Art, 'photography is painting writ small'. We have instant subject matter surrounding us, over-the-counter materials, and if we want it – an available mass-circulation media, but millions of images are made then to vanish into the bottomless void of photography's past never to emerge again. Apart from a Cartier-Bresson or a Diane Arbus or a Richard Avedon, none of us could claim, with any confidence, that we could recognise an individual photographer's work. There seems no obvious authorship involved in this particular 'art'. Photojournalists, advertising and fashion photographers – opinion formers and social documenters – have little concern for their personal signature, and only a lucky few are later republished, usually in new formats, their work rescaled and edited. The European-based 'human-interest' style, the early Modern Movement internationalism from the 1920s, the celebrity portrait collection – all have been revisited and embellished in handsome volumes with new contexts and fancy introductions.

Publishers, photographic galleries and historians have discriminated against certain types of photographic practice and supported, I suppose, the commercially conservative and easily familiar. Universally, architectural photography has never been respectable,

No one would have believed, in the last years of the nineteen
century, that human affairs were being watched keenly and close
by intelligences greater than man's and yet as mortal as his ow
that as men busied themselves about their affairs they we
scrutinized and studied, perhaps almost as narrowly as a ma
with a microscope might scrutinize the transient creatures th
swarm and multiply in drops of water. ● With infina
complacency men went to and fro over this globe about their litt
affairs, serene in their assurance of their empire over matter. It
possible that the infusoria under the microscope do the same. N
one gave a thought to the older worlds of space as sources
human danger, or thought of them only to dismiss the idea of li
upon them as impossible and improbable. It is curious to reca
some of the mental habits of those departed days. At mos
terrestrial men fancied there might be other men upon Mar
perhaps inferior to themselves and ready to welcome a missiona
enterprise. Yet, across the gulf of space, minds that are to ou
minds as ours are to those of the beasts that perish, intellects va
and cool and unsympathetic, regarded this earth with enviou
eyes, and slowly and surely drew their plans against us. And ear
in the twentieth century came the great disillusionment. Th
planet Mars, I scarcely need remind listeners, revolves about th
sun at a mean distance of 140,000,000 miles, and the light ar
heat it receives from the sun is barely half of that received by th
world. It must be, if the nebular hypothesis has any truth, old
than our world, and long before this earth ceased to be molten, li
upon its surface must have begun its course. The fact that it
scarcely one-seventh of the volume of the earth must ha
accelerated its cooling to the temperature at which life cou
begin. It has air and water, and all that is necessary for th
support of animated existence.

HG Wells 1898 | Orson Welles 1938 The War of The Worlds.
Poster Malcolm Frost | Igma London 2004

its problems or solutions rarely understood and promoted. Although at the birth of our invention, architecture was the main subject of focus, because obviously buildings didn't move around or fidget in front of the pioneers' clumsy equipment. From the 1850s to the Farm Security Administration programme at the end of the 1930s, huge photographic surveys were commissioned and undertaken, making nonsense of the claims that photography was somehow inconsequential and banal. The main subject was architectural. Architecture was not only passive, but within its surfaces and spaces it contained human history, our art and decoration, politics, philosophies, ingenuity and experimentation.

Architecture dealt with time. The camera was the only vehicle that could pass through a building, or indeed an environment, and record its spatial qualities with absolute truthfulness. The hand-held photographic eye, stopping and recording; moving and recording again – the floor, ceiling, from above and below; through the space; its relationship to its built neighbourhood; its relationship to humankind – the micro to the macro. The still camera was the medium to express the art and structure of architecture.

Unlike all other forms of artistic expression, the photographic print was the only convincing way of communicating the truth of a building. Not only in hard information terms – an essential as far as the successful architectural photograph is concerned – but the spirit of place. A small architectural detail in the hands of the master architectural photographer Judith Turner can evoke in the viewer's mind vast, complicated form. A cityscape by Paolo Rosselli, shot kilometres away from his actual subject, can suggest an eternity – the unending curvature of our planet itself.

Later on in this section are posters advertising the photographic work of Rosselli, Ohashi, Neves and Morley Von Sternberg. Von Sternberg, Neves and

Rosselli were for Volume Gallery exhibitions and the Margolies for the Building Centre. All five photographers have a complete understanding of the unique problems that shooting architecture entails. They all solve these difficulties, with their own individual charm, wonderfully well. The designer's real difficulty is treating their work with 'kid-gloves'.

Designers should be confident in themselves to do what they will with any photographer's image. The poster's problem is that it has to be seen first, and make the curious 'buy' the product. This is a very special – art/ commercial/ seduction/ communication/ competition problem – and the designer should feel free to use any device available. We all treat art with an almost religious respect, as if it's outside life itself, but the designer of publicity works with different criteria – our work must get people into the show. The problem (for designers) always comes when, after papering the walls with their best shot and with the client's money, no one turns up.

The poster for Jewish Dialog was for a small-run poetry magazine. The poster for Canadian Writers was for McClelland and Stewart advertising a self help book. Design Workshop designed both in Toronto in 1973.

Some dates, both real and used by artists expressively, remain fixed for all time in our collective consciousness. 1066. 1914-18. 2001. 1984. The 1984 poster was made as a gift for clients and friends.

The Henry Peacock Gallery, London, invited 40 graphic designers to take part in an exhibition of typography, curated by Angharad Lewis and called Public Address System. Designers were asked to pick a speech or quotation from any source and display their choice in a final A2 size. The exhibition was a huge success, both in the quality of the work and attendance numbers. My contribution was the *War of the Worlds* poster seen at the left.

**115**

TITIAN, PORTRAIT OF A MAN. C.1492

JOHN HOYLAND. NEW YEAR'S DAY 1981

Western Art

Renaissance
to the present.

An exhibition
of books and
periodicals.

Arranged by
the British
Council.

116

Henry Peacock Gallery
38a Foley Street
London W1P 7LB
tel:+ 44(0)207 323 4033
info@henrypeacock.com
www.henrypeacock.com
open: Wed-Sat 12-6pm

**Henry Peacock Gallery**

JOS-DB
270B 65

Henry Peacock Gallery
**The Josephine Baker House | Dan Brady**

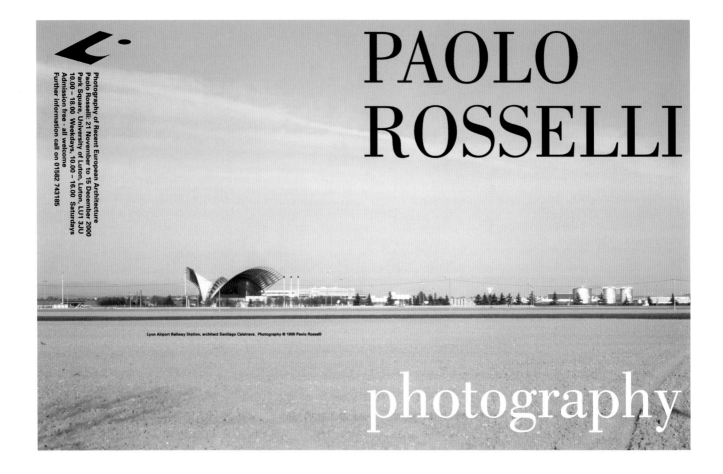

118

"THE PERFECT ILLUSION"
Exhibitions on the History of
Photography & Cinematography
Harrogate Festival 5-18 August.

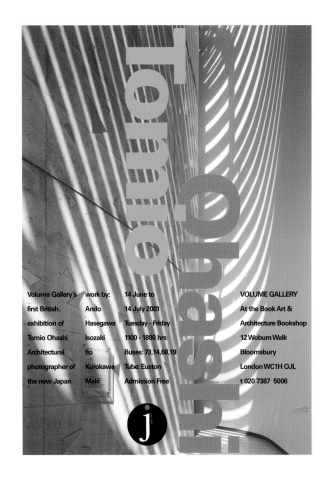

| | | | |
|---|---|---|---|
| Volume Gallery's | work by: | 14 June to | VOLUME GALLERY |
| first British | Ando | 14 July 2001 | At the Book Art & |
| exhibition of | Hasegawa | Tuesday - Friday | Architecture Bookshop |
| Tomio Ohashi | Isozaki | 1100 - 1800 hrs | 12 Wobum Walk |
| Architectural | Ito | Buses: 73,14,68,19 | Bloomsbury |
| photographer of | Kurokawa | Tube: Euston | London WC1H OJL |
| the new Japan | Maki | Admission Free | t 020 7387 5006 |

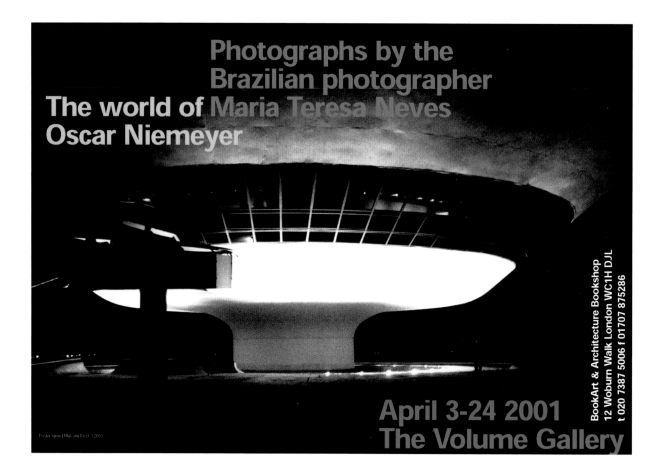

Photographs by the
Brazilian photographer
The world of Maria Teresa Neves
Oscar Niemeyer

April 3-24 2001
The Volume Gallery

BookArt & Architecture Bookshop
12 Woburn Walk London WC1H DJL
t 020 7387 5006 f 01707 875286

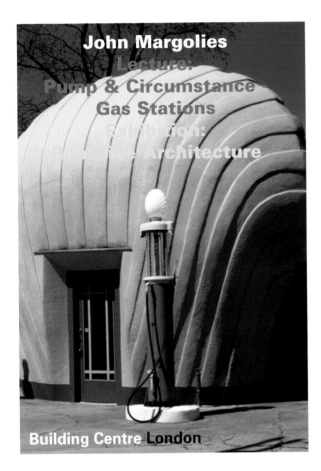

**John Margolies**
Lecture:
Pump & Circumstance
Gas Stations
Exhibition:
Architecture

**Building Centre London**

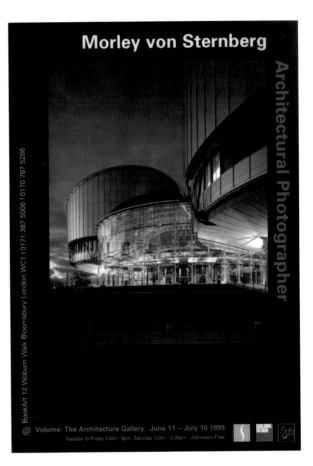

**Morley von Sternberg**

Architectural Photographer

BookArt 12 Woburn Walk Bloomsbury London WC1 t 0171 387 5006 f 0170 787 5286

@ **Volume: The Architecture Gallery. June 11 – July 10 1999**
Tuesday to Friday 11am - 6pm  Saturday 11am - 2.30pm   Admission Free

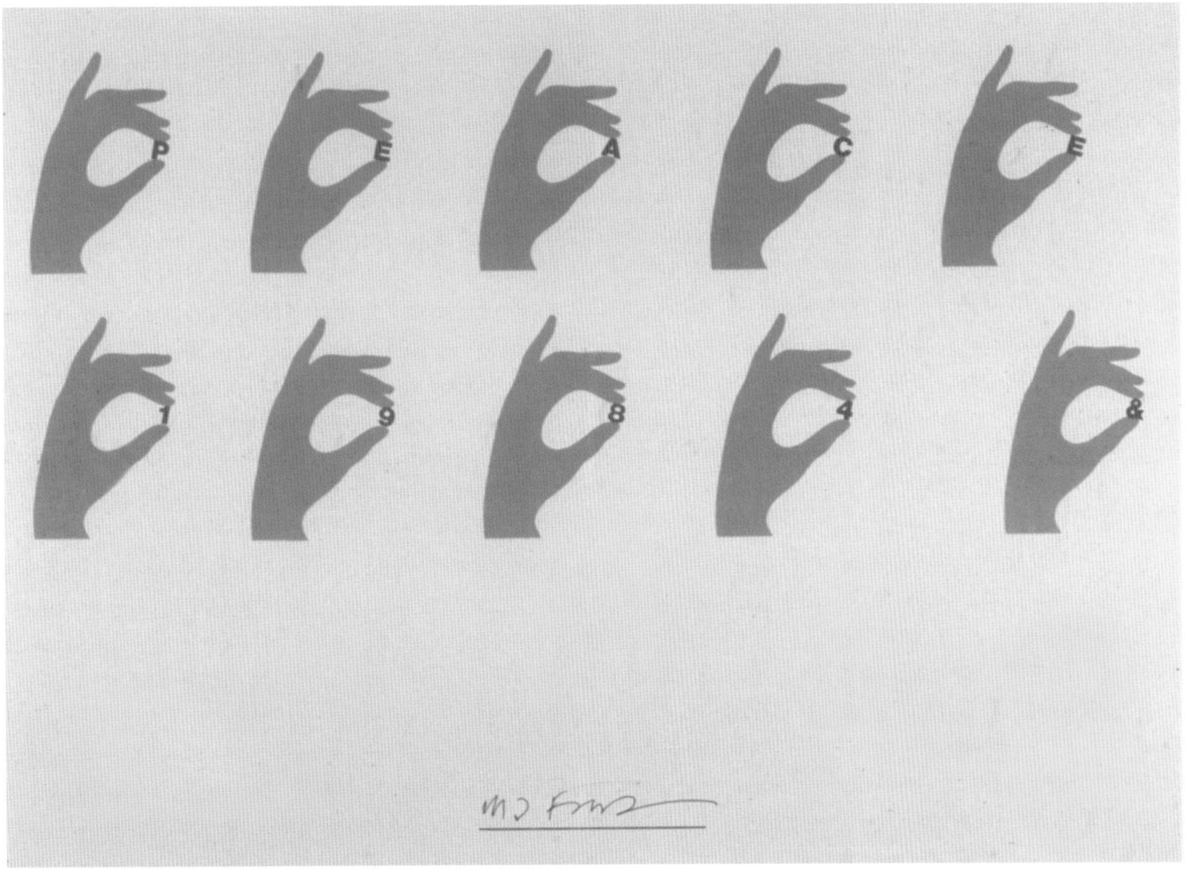
P
E
A
C
E
1
9
8
4
&

# Florentine Flower Show | Catherine Slessor

In a world of increasing information saturation, how do you represent a city? By its buildings, monuments or famous residents? In some cases, a city can be represented and even branded quite simply through a graphic cipher – the winged lion of Venice or Berlin's bear, perhaps. But there are few more familiar and deeply ingrained city symbols than the fleur-de-lis of Florence. Adorning every conceivable surface like floral confetti, the distinctive red lily on a white ground that has been the city's symbol since its foundation, is truly omnipresent. From litter bins to menus, manhole covers to police helmets, cafe awnings to souvenirs, even on the purple shirts of Fiorentina, the local soccer team known affectionately as *i gigliati* (the lilies), the little red fleur-de-lis is a constant indicator of civic pride and local identity.

The graphic quality of this hyper-abundant flower varies enormously. Sometimes it is meticulously and floridly rendered down to the last quivering stamen, at other times the triumvirate of delicately curled petals is brutally abstracted to a simple trident, serving both the needs of municipal functionalism and the lightning scrawl of the graffiti artist. Like all memorable symbols, it compresses a welter of myth, culture and allusion into an arresting visual device, but it also resonates more profoundly with Florentine culture, emblematic of the city's devotion to the cult of the Virgin Mary.

Few heraldic and symbolic emblems have had such an intriguing and lengthy history as the fleur-de-lis (literally 'flower of the lily'). Its origins extend back into the mists of antiquity and early priests and the religious scholars accepted its quasi-mystical qualities without question. The lily is said to have sprung from the tears shed by Eve as she left Eden and from earliest times has been a potent symbol of feminine purity, humility, devotion and divinity. Accordingly it was readily adopted by the Christian church as an attribute of the Virgin Mary, and makes regular appearances in paintings, sculpture and altarpieces. In depictions of the annunciation, the Angel Gabriel often proffers a white lily to the young Mary, or the flower is seen standing in a vase, another symbol of the feminine principal.

The Feast of the Annunciation on 25th March was a major Florentine feast day and the Marian cult reached its height with the building of Santa Maria del Fiore (Mary of the Flowers), Florence's magnificent Renaissance cathedral crowned with its great dome (yet another feminine principal) designed by Filippo Brunelleschi.

The distinctive tri-petal Florentine fleur-de-lis was originally a white lily on a red field, but in the mid 13th century the rebellious Guelphs drove the ruling Ghibellin faction out of the city and in a fit of yah-boo triumph, the colours were inverted to a red lily on a white shield, the symbol that persists to this day. Academics, botanists and heraldic experts continue to argue about the exact genus of the flower (some claim it is actually more of an iris than lily, as irises grew naturally on the city walls and also symbolise feminine purity), but as the images on the following pages show, Florence and the Florentines have become inseparable from their fleur-de-lis, now energetically reinterpreted for modern city life.

1956-69

Fiorentina A.C. È un'esclusiva Basic Merchandise. Torino Italy

1940-61
66-75

1960-61

A C
F

Fiorentina

Catherine Slessor is an architect and
managing editor of *The Architectural
Review*. She regularly contributes to
European and American design magazines
and is the author of several books including
*Eco Tech-High Technology*, *Sustainable
Architecture* and *Concrete Regionalism*.
She lives in London.

# Buildings that talk | Catherine Slessor

The physical fabric of a city can be used for much larger graphic gestures than the Florentine fleur-de-lis. Buildings can be used as billboards, in the conventional sense as locations for advertising hoardings or, more interestingly, can themselves be transformed into sites of super-size graphics, bearing messages that cajole, proclaim, entreat, emote or simply bemuse. The practice is not new; the portico of the ancient Pantheon in Rome bears a long thin inscription, like carved tickertape, by the Emperor Hadrian dedicating the temple to his predecessor Agrippa. In the 1920s, Rodchenko and the poet Mayakovsy (as copywriter) conceived the advertising for Mossel'prom (Moscow agricultural industry) and had it painted on the building in the centre of Moscow – turgidity on a massive scale.

Swiss architects Herzog and de Meuron regularly write, project or print letters and images on their buildings and Dutch architects Neutelings Riedjik covered the façade of a print works in individual, evenly spaced letters that if read in a certain way constituted a poem. Paula Scher, principal of Pentagram New York has asserted that 'cities are like magazines' and enjoys splashing monumental lettering all over the American built environment. One flank of Cardiff's new concert hall incorporates giant 'chiselled' lettering on a scale so Brobdinagian, the inscription, which glows at night, could be read from miles away. Another particularly memorable example of Falstaffian excess was the number nine (10 feet high and bright red) designed by Chermayeff and Geismar in the 1970s that marked the entrance to the Solon Building Company Headquarters at 9 West 57th Street in New York. Apparently, neither the client nor the city welcomed its presence. Hyperbole is a defining characteristic of our current era. Everything is a 'masterpiece'; every major city is the 'greatest on earth'; every personal goal has to be 'the most difficult, costly, spectacular or courageous' ever known. We live in a Barnum and Bailey world, full of huckstering feats that overcome impossible odds. We roar to gain attention, dress to get noticed and turn cartwheels to stand out. Some public advertising is so large that it requires its own scaffolding, like a real building, to physically secure its message against the elements. Public buildings often use typographic signs and images, electronic or otherwise, as part of their façades. Las Vegas has become a cliché, overtaken by the hyperactivity of Tokyo's Shibuya district, a saturated netherworld of light and colour, where meaningless words and slogans incessantly circulate, seducing and hypnotising passers by.

We have come a long way from making sense of 6-point unleaded reading matter to attempting to digest King Kong typography on Billy Bunter buildings. The appalling indecipherable and non-communicative graphic chaos found everywhere on our streets has encouraged some architects and their graphic collaborators to respond with 'buildings that talk'. Today, we need to be seen in order to be heard. Our amazing propensity for attention seeking and spectacular showing off is fed by a need to advertise whenever and wherever we can. The human fallacy of all this excess is that we are unable to get beyond our own physical scale, limited vision and preoccupied minds. We cannot see, let alone apprehend, towering messages designed for Gargantua or Godzilla. Every competing graphic device, whether in 40-foot high lettering or an A5 poster for a missing budgie, forms part of an overwhelming visual mush.

**131**

Opposite page 133:
Shopping centre, Lisbon, Portugal.
Photograph Sergio Guerra 2004.

Veenman Printworks
Building, Ede, The Netherlands.
Photograph Christian Richters 2005.

Welsh Millennium Centre
Cardiff Bay, Wales.
Photograph Raf Makda/VIEW 2005.

We are all experiencing, more and
more frequently, new buildings that
have something to say. The
examples we show here from The
Netherlands, Wales and Portugal,
use huge lettering – painted, pierced
and three-dimensional; 76-foot-high
letters that few will see or read or
memorise.

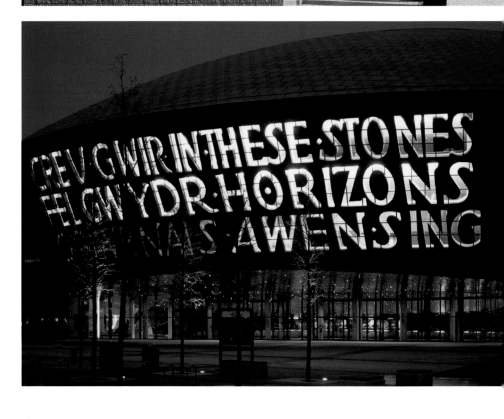

# MIKE LEIGH   IN CONVERSATION

The poster for Impact found on page 137, advertised the first issue of the *Canadian Cinema* magazine. The magazine was given away free, in cinemas in Ontario, to all paying customers. Advertising paid for design, staff and printing and so on. Design Workshop was commissioned to design the identity, the contents and the promotion for this monthly. The magazine lasted a few years before the owners moved into other theatrical and cinematic ventures and eventually closed.

In 1986 the British Council's film department asked me to design a series of posters advertising live interviews and film packages featuring three British filmmakers. Both Derek Jarman, who was extremely ill at the time of his interview, and Lindsay Anderson, in a silly swimming accident, died soon after the promotion was publicly available. Mike Leigh is still fine and alive – he received a Golden Lion award at the 2004 Venice Film Festival for *Vera Drake*. John Cartwright, the department's senior executive, planned the series and whether it continued beyond the initial trio of directors I don't know.

Mike Leigh was born in 1943, in Salford, Manchester. His distinctive and distinguished work is based on a series of acting improvisations – often using the same group of players. His early theatre work has successfully transferred to cinema and television, and he is now one of Europe's leading directors.

Lindsay Anderson (born in Bangalore, 1923) joined the English Stage Company at the Royal Court Theatre in 1957, after studying at Oxford University and directing documentary films (*Thursday's Children* – won an Oscar). His great success came through his caustic view of the Establishment. A favourite Anderson insult about anything poorly done or made was 'It's so English.'

Derek Jarman was a Londoner (born 1942) and studied painting at the Slade School of Art. He worked as a set and costume designer before making his first feature film in 1976. Jarman directed pop-videos, designed for opera and ballet, wrote several books (including *Dancing Ledge*, his autobiography) as well as making beautiful movies. All three directors are wonderful examples of how the British can produce creative magic when the determination of the individual cuts through all the compromises of money, market, status quo and the cultural mores of *The Daily Mail*.

In 1987 the British Film Institute asked me to design posters to advertise two of their books. Eisenstein, one of the world's great filmmakers, was born in Riga, Latvia in 1898. He was a scene painter in various theatres before developing his characteristic, impressionistic cinema effects. He is renowned for skilful cutting and group and crowd surging movement. The book is the first part of a three-volume edition of Eisenstein's writing and letters. The typography was the same in all three, apart from different colour-ways, the background writing and the 'film-strip' changed and the three books could fit together, on display, as a kind of historical film-frieze.

Yasujiro Ozu was born in Tokyo in 1903 and died there in his 60th year. As a young man he visited the cinema three or four times a week, and became an assistant cameraman in his teens. Ozu's films are gentle, funny and compassionate but latterly were laced with tragedy. A still from his most famous film *Tokyo Story* is shown in the grey background. The lettering was drawn on a flag, photographed and then reversed out.

The image for The Berlin Film Festival is of Helen Mirren featured in a movie-drama about the Irish troubles.

January 1972

"Impact"
"The Canadian Cinema Magazine"
Premier Issue

Nicholas and Alexandra and the
Romanov Massacre; the real story, maybe

Frank Zappa in one of his 200 motels
Peter Boyle on Peter Boyle
Finding McCabe's coat in Toronto

plus Gerald Pratley, Earl Pomerantz, George Anthony
and the movies you'll be seeing in the next month

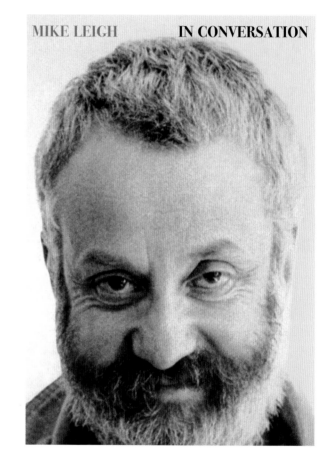

MIKE LEIGH          IN CONVERSATION

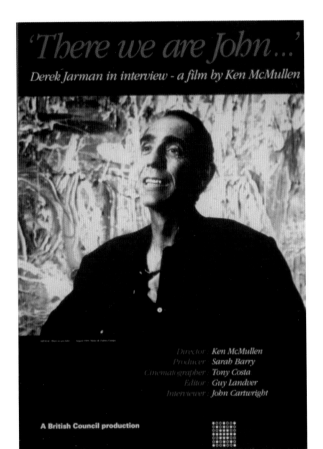

'There we are John...'

Derek Jarman in interview - a film by Ken McMullen

Director : Ken McMullen
Producer : Sarah Barry
Cinematographer : Tony Costa
Editor : Guy Landver
Interviewer : John Cartwright

A British Council production

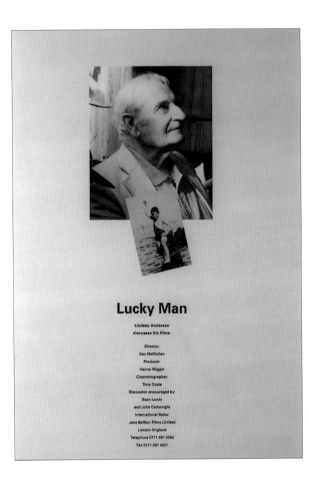

## Lucky Man

Lindsay Anderson
discusses his films.

Director:
Ken McMullen
Producer:
Hanna Wiggin
Cinematographer:
Tony Costa
Discussion encouraged by:
Sean Lewis
and John Cartwright
International Sales:
Jane Balfour Films Limited
London England
Telephone 0171 287 0392
Fax 0171 287 4241

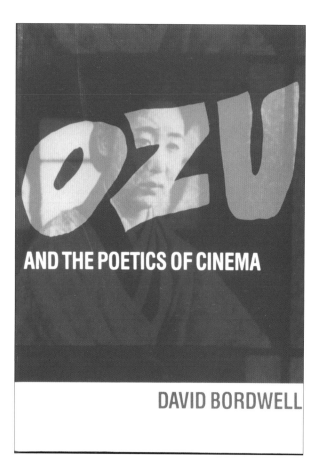

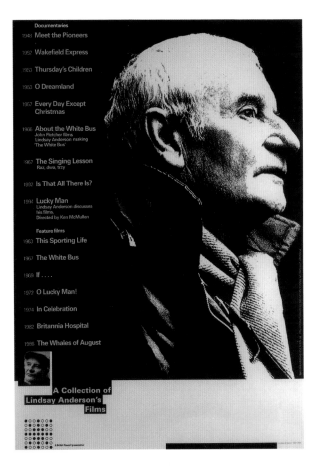

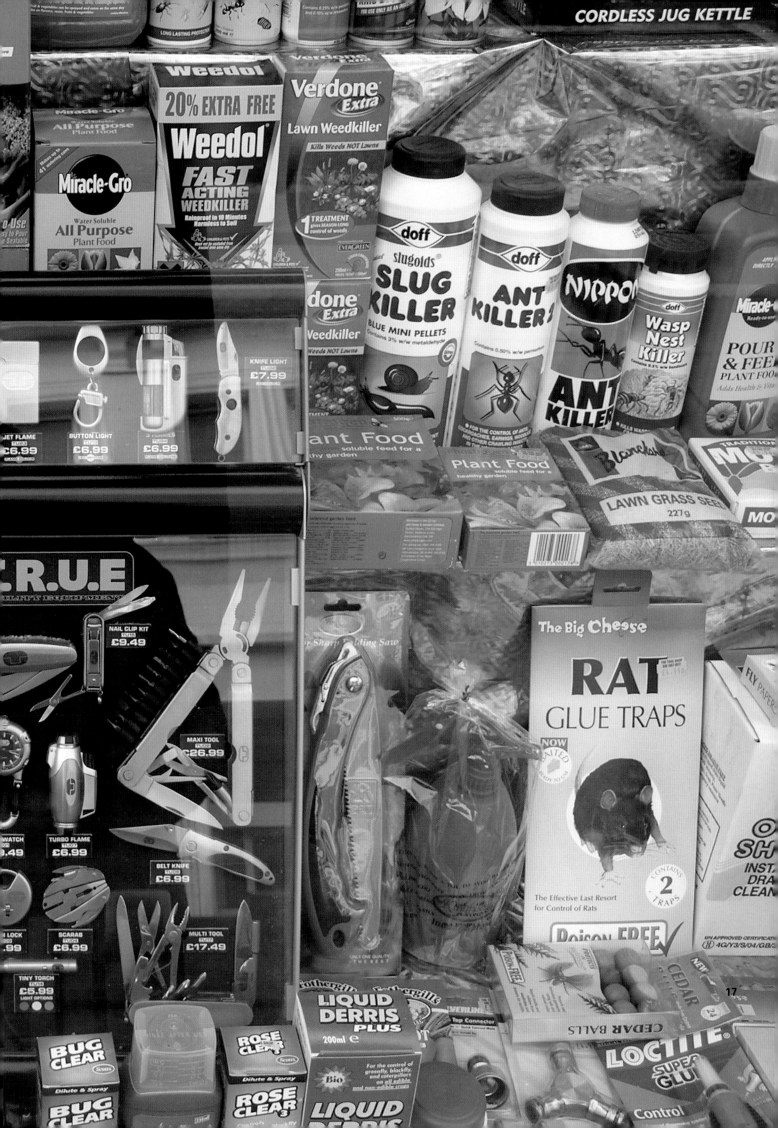

AAT

# TERROR IN QUEBEC

## Case studies of the FLQ

Gustave Morf

The Building Centre is located in one of London's most important half square miles. To the west is the hugely mixed commercial shopping street, Tottenham Court Road, containing Habitat and other 'designer' stores. To the south lies The British Museum, Bedford Square, the Architectural Association, and to the east London University. Hotels and student accommodation and Russell Square lie to the north. The Centre supplies information to anyone that wishes to know about building materials, function and manufacture and availability.

They offer a continuously updated service of printed information, live displays and personal expert advice on every aspect of the building industry for professionals and non-professionals alike, for free. The Building Centre Trust administers The Centre and also manages various events, exhibitions, seminars etc., to attract a constant supply of visitors to The Centre itself. Our client is The Building Centre Trust and what follows are a few of our posters for their events. Apart from a logotype the Trust has no graphic identity, so all the posters are treated as if they are advertising one-off events. As well as *Trial & Error* and *Yes we can!*, we made posters and an exhibition device for a series of exhibitions called Super Models. We show the poster advertising the sports show.

The poster for Paul Rudolph, also for The Building Centre Trust, advertised a book launch and an exhibition designed by Dennis Crompton of Archigram that ran for a month in early 2000.

*Trial & Error* was seen between 20 May and 5 July 2003. The ideas of thirteen architects were displayed within a special installation, designed by Magma Architecture and Buro Happold – using 31mm cardboard that looked like a gigantic paper model itself. The main graphic used on the A0 poster shows a computer sketch of the exhibition layout. We also designed an exhibition logotype using three weights of Univers. All the publicity material was printed in black.

In October we designed the poster, invitations and the exhibition device for *Yes We Can!* a live show promoting three workshops.

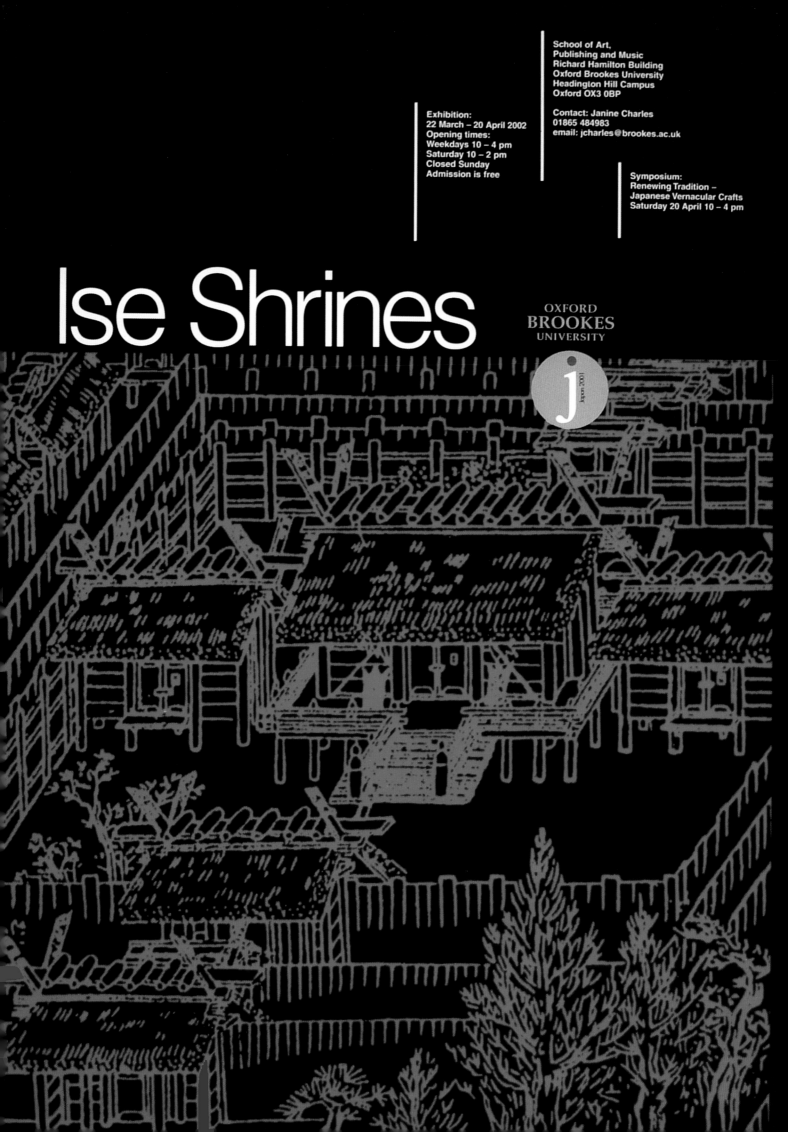

School of Art,
Publishing and Music
Richard Hamilton Building
Oxford Brookes University
Headington Hill Campus
Oxford OX3 0BP

Exhibition:
22 March – 20 April 2002
Opening times:
Weekdays 10 – 4 pm
Saturday 10 – 2 pm
Closed Sunday
Admission is free

Contact: Janine Charles
01865 484983
email: jcharles@brookes.ac.uk

Symposium:
Renewing Tradition –
Japanese Vernacular Crafts
Saturday 20 April 10 – 4 pm

# Ise Shrines

OXFORD
BROOKES
UNIVERSITY

j  Japan 2001

Ise Shrines, was for an exhibition and symposium at an Oxford college. We threw the typography together and let the wonderful Japanese engraving do the work for us. The Japan 2002 circular symbol plus the centred Oxford Brookes thing was placed blindfold. Students stole all the exhibited posters and the print run had to be repeated.

The Aga Khan Awards for Architecture are given triennially for excellence in architecture for Muslim cultures. The scope ranges from local improvement schemes through restoration to all kinds of contemporary buildings. The jury, internationally known figures, meet twice, first to see recommended work then to make final short-listed awards. The prize money is divided equally between the awards and is distributed between the people responsible for the building. We made the full-colour poster and repeated the square device for the invitation, with 12 squares being die-cut out of the front.

Spa Green was a Volume Gallery show with no money. The show was about the life of a Clerkenwell block of flats, and was touching and warm. The cheaply printed poster, I think, give a false view of the flats – but is an interesting piece of graphic design. (Hans Schleger was right about rushing time – we should have made something more colourful and friendly and more appropriate).

Michael Bullock is an elderly poet and surrealist picture maker living in Canada. The exhibition of his work was held at Volume Gallery in 2003, and the poster features his drawing techniques.

Finally the FLQ design was a parody of one of my favourite posters: Brian Tattersfield's American in Paris (for the Royal College's film society) with the Coke bottle replaced by a Molotov cocktail. And Frost/Milton designed it in Toronto in the 1970s. Freedom fighters or terrorists whatever you call them – the innocent always die.

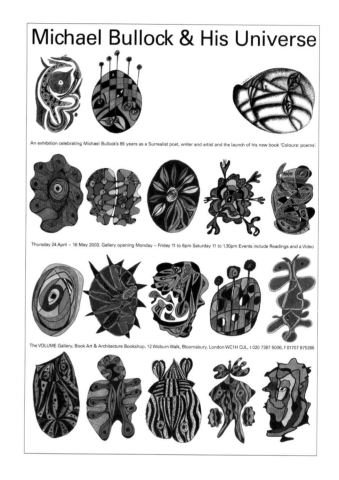

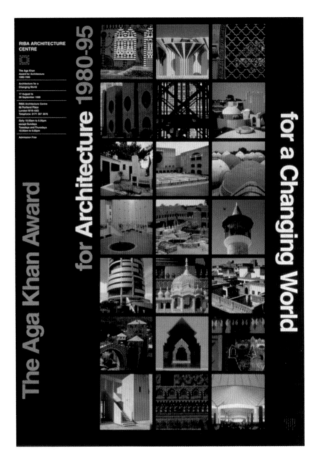

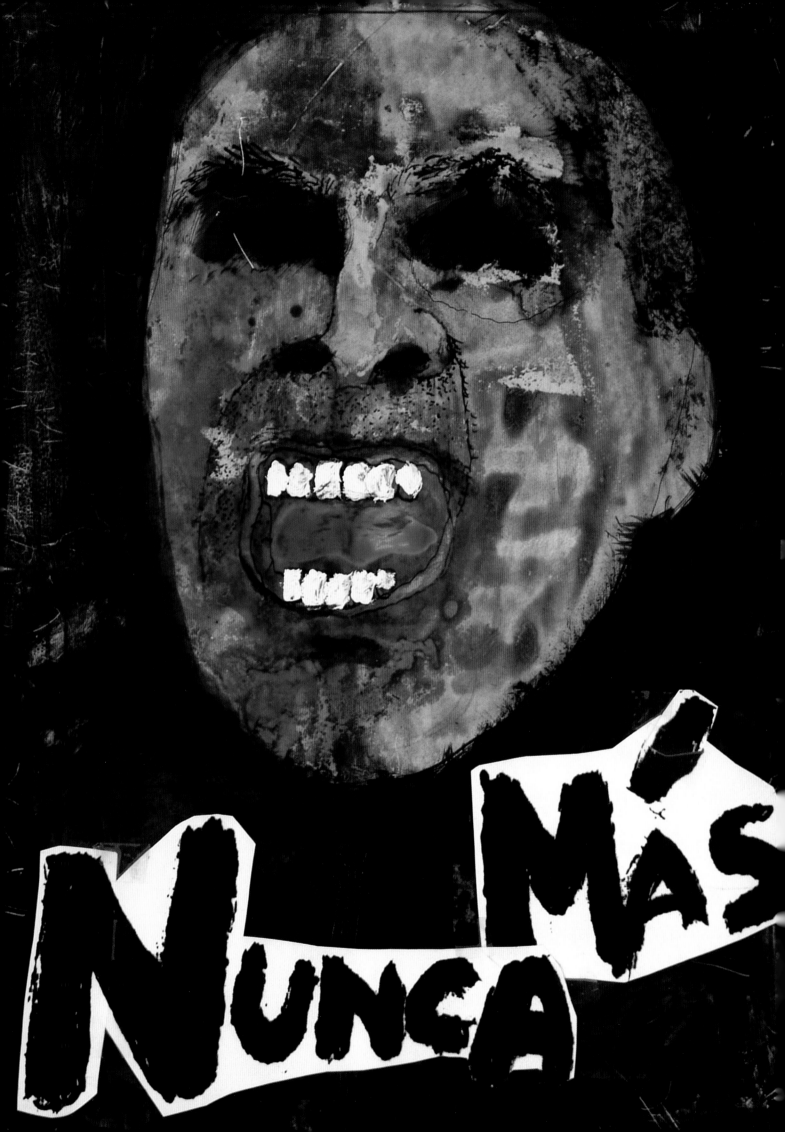

The poster on the left was made for the visit of Gustavo Pinochet (for health reasons) and was rejected for the Public Address System exhibition, previously mentioned in this book.

Thames Television employed me in their early days as design director in the promotion department. (The entire department consisted of the writer Mike Loftus and myself). The poster advertising the Steven Frears' directed programme about poverty in the St Ann's area of Nottingham, was banned by the Thames TV directors because the programme condemned a Labour Party election promise about building thousands of new homes. The broadcast went out on air but without publicity. 1969 political censorship. The football score line is genuine. The idea was that winning the Pools was the only feasible escape from the localised poverty trap. The Vietnam poster is powerfully direct, and was substantiated with other forms of promotion. The war and its horrors were covered everywhere and was hugely emotive – so the image, typeface and layout of this poster could not fail to hold the attention.

Alexsei Gan was a poster that should be promoting a book that never happened. Catherine Cooke, a distinguished scholar of Russian arts and architecture, and I were in the process of bringing Alexsei

Gan out of the shadows, when Catherine had her tragic accident. The book was written and designed, The Images Publishing Group was going to publish, but now with Catherine's untimely death, the whole project is, sadly, no longer viable.

The aristocratic-looking Russian is Alexsei Gan working from a photograph by his dear friend Aleksandr Rodchenko. Gan, before he was murdered by Stalin's police system, was a catalyst for most design strands of the Revolution. (The Russian word just spells the name Gan).

He was born in 1893 and died in 1940 in a labour camp. He was a close associate of Malevich and made photomontage experiments in 1918. He published the Constructivist Treatise in 1922 and was editor of *Sovremennaya Arkhitektura (CA)*. Gan designed film posters, kiosks, he wrote plays, he was an orator, organiser, a friend to every avant-garde Russian designer you have ever heard of. Hopefully his life will be published one day, and one missing name from a great artistic revolution will be made available to us all.

The parody of Jan Tschichold's promotion of Die Neue Typographie using Goebbels' Fire Speech was made in collaboration with Thom Winterburn and exhibited at the Public Address System exhibition.

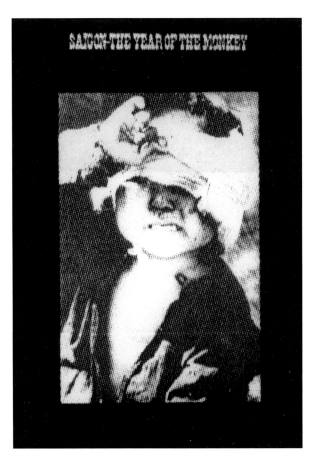

SAIGON-THE YEAR OF THE MONKEY

# Nottingham Forest 0 Arsenal 2.

Tonight's Report on ITV is about poverty in Nottingham. About people who live in a slum district called St Ann's.

People like Mrs Churchill whose only chance of escape is a win on the football pools.

Tonight she talks about life in St Ann's. A claustrophobic community of 30,000 people.

Where the pawn shop is the bank, the public wash-house a social club.

St Ann's is not the only slum district in Nottingham. And Nottingham is not the only city in Britain with a housing problem.

But that's no comfort to the people you'll see tonight. Or to those you won't see.

Report: 10.30 tonight on ITV

**THAMES**
Thames Television Television House London

**NEUE ORDNUNG**

For PUBLIC ADDRESS SYSTEM exhibition at the Henry Peacock Gallery London
Poster Speeches by 40 typographers 9.1.04 - 14.2.04

## JOSEPH GOEBBELS
The Ministry of Public Enlightenment and Propaganda. Mob Orator and Nazi Servant

# DIE FEURREDE

**May 10 1933. Deutsche Stattsoper, Berlin –
the regime consigned decadent works to the flames**

Deutsche Studenten: Wir haben unsere Handeln gegen den undeutschen Geist gerichtet; übergebt alles undeutschen dem Feuer, gegen Klassenkampf und Materialismus, für Volksgemeinschaft und idealistische Lebenshaltung. Ich übergebe dem Feuer die Schriften von **Karl Marx und Kautsky.**

Gegen Dekadenz und moralischen Verfall! Für Zucht und Sitte in Familie und Staat! Ich übergebe dem Feuer die Schriften von **Heinrich Mann, Glaeser, Erich Kästner.**

Gegen Gesinnungslumperei und politischen Verrat, für Hingabe an Volk und Staat! Ich übergebe dem Feuer die Schriften des **Friedrich Wilhelm Förster.**

Gegen seelenzerfassende Überschätzung des Trieblebens, für den Adel der menschlichen Seele! Ich übergebe dem Feuer die Schriften des **Sigmund Freud.**

Gegen Verfälschung unserer Geschichte und Herabwürdigung ihrer großen Gestalten, für Ehrfurcht vor unserer Vergangenheit! Ich übergebe dem Feuer die Schriften des **Emil Ludwig Kohn und Werner Hegemann.**

Gegen volksfremden Journalismus demokratisch-jüdischer Prägung, für verantwortungsbewusste Mitarbeit am Werk des nationalen Aufbaus! Ich übergebe dem Feuer die Schriften des **Theodor Wolff und Bernhard.**

Gegen literarischen Verrat am Soldaten des Weltkrieges, für Erziehung des Volkes im Geist der Wahrhaftigkeit! Ich übergebe dem Feuer die Schriften des **Remarque.**

Gegen dünkelhafte Verhunzung der deutschen Sprache, für Pflege des kostbarsten Gutes unseres Volkes! Ich übergebe dem Feuer die Schriften des **Alfred Kerr.**

Gegen Frechheit und Anmaßung, für Achtung und Ehrfurcht vor dem unsterblichen deutschen Volksgeist. Verschlinge, Feuer, auch Schriften der **Tucholsky, Ossietzky!**

Against class conflict, I hand over the writings of Karl Marx and Kautsky to the fire. For political betrayal, I hand over the writings of Friedrich Wilhelm Förster to the fire. For the aristocracy of the human soul, I hand over the writings of Freud to the fire. For respect for our past, I hand over the writings of Kohn and Hegemann to the fire. Against Jewish-democratic-influenced journalism, I hand over the writings of Wolff and Bernhard to the fire. For literary betrayal of our soldiers I hand over the writings of Remarque to the fire. **Against the debasement of the German language** I hand over the writings of Kerr to the fire. Devour fire, the work of Tucholsky & Ossietzky!

**GOEBBELS OR GOBBELS**

(Paul) Joseph [Goebels] 1897-1945 politician
b. Rheydt Germany
Deformed foot absolved him from military service
Anti-semite
As youth attended many universities
Powerful exponent of the radical aspects of Nazi philosophy. When Hitler was running the war Goebbels was running the country.

**The unacceptable to the new order**
Albert Einstein
Sigmund Freud
Erich Maria Remarque
Carl von Ossietzky
Kurt Tucholsky
Hugo von Hofmannsthal
Erich Kästner
Carl Zuckmayer
Karl Marx etc
Bertolt Brecht wrote a poem Die Bücherverbrennung (The Book Burning) demanding that the regime burn him, since it had not burnt his writings and so he was therefore denied this incendiary public recognition.

'Where books
are burnt in the end people are also burnt'
**Heinrich Heine**

**The New Typography (Berlin 1928) A Modern Handbook:** was the vision of a man from Leipzig who was convinced that his beliefs were the only truth, and that the sooner they were recognized by everyone the better and purer life would be. It was also necessary to sweep away the 'rubbish' of the past.

info@henrypeacock.com. Telephone 020 7323 4033
TO
Gallery opening Wednesday to Saturday only
PM

**12.**00

**6.**00

➡️

Organiser Angharad Lewis

Tienez,

FRED IS FUN!

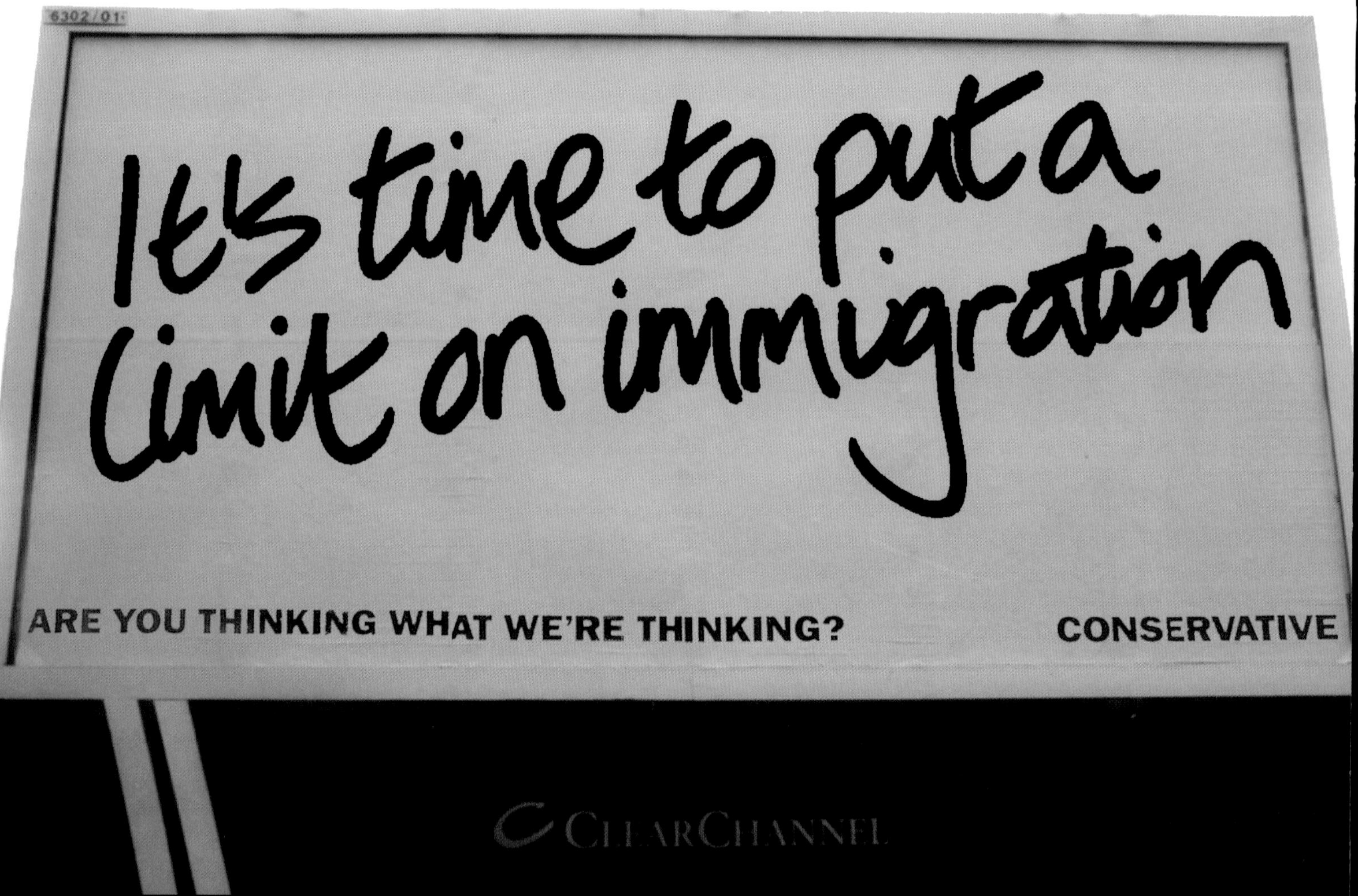
It's time to put a limit on immigration
ARE YOU THINKING WHAT WE'RE THINKING?
CONSERVATIVE
CLEARCHANNEL

I was walking through the park yesterday and happened to walk over a scrawled message on the path that announced 'don't go to work.' I dismissed this as the disaffected ex-students of the area encouraging their brethren in their collective listlessness and apathy or perhaps it was some political call-to-arms by some naïve leftist reminding us of the alienation of labour. A few steps later, I saw the graffiti had a punchline – 'I'm talking to you Dean'. Somehow this changed the communication from a generalised announcement to a more pointed and specific address to a friend. I imagine the ex-student reluctantly making his way across the park at seven in the morning to find this satirical, and yet affectionate plea to the work-shy and/or alienated worker.

At the same time I watch on TV the new advert for Apple's ipod/itunes service seeing the ultimate young 20-something walking through the city (New York City because it's always New York City in our heads) past a hoarding containing a series of posters which become animated the very moment the young man walks past them, oblivious to the world around him with his IPod providing a soundtrack to his flaneur-like drift. There is something fitting in the idea of browsing – this suggests ultimate choice – through your IPod's thousands of tunes, of browsing in a disinterested and anonymous manner through the city, of browsing cyberspace.

Again in *Minority Report*, Spielberg enlisted the top futurologist minds at MIT to predict future trends (doesn't this spell something of a lack of confidence in Philip K Dick's powers of invention?). Tom Cruise is seen negotiating his way through a mall (the mall will never die in the future) and each successive interactive poster addresses him directly by name. On my computer I go to Amazon and it uncannily has settled on the right DVD and CD for me. I want to react and buy a Girls Aloud album or walk through town backwards. To throw the computer controlled CCTV off the scent.

Somehow I hope that this behaviour might fry the server's computational brain, that it fails to cope with the naturally contradictory and idiosyncratic human behaviour. But I fear I have simply defined another 'niche' that I now belong to a new bolshie demographic who enjoy walking backwards that some marketer is at that very moment sending a field researcher to define or who is trying to explain this to an advertising agency who are in the process of pitching an ad for anti-cynicism cream – with extra AHA's (isn't that the richest piece of irony?) and fruit radicals – to this demographic (that's who put graphic in demographic).

The poster has always had a wider constituency. The poster by its very nature implies a mass urban society, whether this is the early posters printed to publicise quack medical cures, circuses, freaks and runaway servants or the streets of Paris as photographed by the likes of Atget and Nadar, walls covered in posters for cafe-concerts or the subsequent work of those such as Cheret and Lautrec in their 'art' lithographs for the new urban amusements of the music hall etc. Part of their lure and seduction lay in the very way they addressed a mass audience that actively promenaded the streets of the modern city, whether this was Haussmann's remodelled Paris or the slum-cleared streets of the West-End of London. By the turn of the century, a commentator like Blaise Cendrars was able to proclaim that the billboard was a 'cathedral of sensuality.' (It's interesting that this analogy between religion and commerce was made explicit years later when Toscani compared his poster campaigns for Benetton as being like the church's stained-glass windows, using the god of multinational capital for social ends by informing the population about AIDS, genocide, racism etc.) The poster was synonymous with a mass street culture. It was the modern graphic form.

So what happened? For this book I was talking to an old friend, Malcolm Frost and he decried the death of the poster. Once upon a time (when people say this it seems to always mean the 1960s) a large part of his commissioned work as a graphic designer was poster work, stuff for theatres, arts festivals, government pronouncements. Now this had dried up. Certainly a lot of this work came from public money (from particular subsidised arts projects, from government, whatever). With the decline of the 'welfare state', with Blairite initiatives mixing public with private money, these forms of public communication have similarly fallen by the wayside. In a provincial city like Leeds, the only notable institution that seems to use the poster is the West Yorkshire Playhouse, whose remit includes the 'widening participation' of a mass audience for the maintenance of their public subsidy. Everywhere else the street is dominated by communications from the private sector (this is of course mirrored by the increasing concern of graphic designers to not be seen as simple instruments or lackeys of multinational capitalism through things like the First Things First Manifesto), exhorting us to buy and consume. So, has the increasing penetration of private money – and all the language/assumptions values expectations that come with this – into the public sphere pushed the old poster out into the margins? It seemed to me that it reflected a noticeable shift and watershed in the conception of this mass urban street culture.

Increasingly over the last 30 years, advertising and marketing has sought out smaller, specific niche audiences, particularly those with expendable income or those that are seen as initiating new trends that might be transferred to more mainstream audiences, mainly youth. Advertising, reflecting new commodity capitalism, has been instrumental in the fragmentation and atomisation of audiences – this has not been an organic process but a considered and conscious attempt to segregate, to identify and exploit. Advertisers went from the old hoary monolithic breakdown of socio-

economic groups (A, B, C1, C2, D and E) to discussions of 'mainstreamers' and 'reformers' to the smaller discrete 'tribes' that are identified today; from broadcasting to 'narrowcasting'.

Through a series of mouse-clicks or through some more immersive and interactive relationship, computer and digital audio-visual technologies today promise to identify the single consumer so that he/she might be targeted more directly with highly personal buying messages. 'You have previously bought iPods and Volkswagens, then you should be interested in buying a Habitat sofa' and so forth.

We might begin to explain this process as starting in the 1960s with the increasing mobility of the working classes, the consumer boom of the early 1960s with its concomitant moral panics about the working classes being seduced by 'the candy-floss world of cheap amusements'. The working class declasses, like my parents, who were educated and/or earned the money to escape the working class but who never felt (or resisted the lure of the) middle-class, those who bought into an oppositional culture that became increasingly commodified in the late 1960s and 1970s, they felt their own uncertain social status very keenly. They needed badges of belonging, of identity. So they bought into of a culture that hated itself and would look anywhere else to appear more cultured and somehow authentic (Conran's fake Provençal dreams). Here was the special consumer. The discerning consumer who needed those badges to mark themselves out as different. The second-generation bohemians who had blazed a trail for an oppositional culture that wasn't left behind completely as they had families and did socially conscientious jobs: the feeling that they were buying something special when they bought reproduction William Morris wallpaper, Sainsburys generic produce, Habitat furniture or *The Guardian*.

And my generation of course defined

itself even more narrowly. In the 1980s we were encouraged to define ourselves purely in terms of the stuff we bought or didn't have the money to afford. These became real badges of identity and meaning – an oppositional culture still existed but was gradually sold off lock, stock and barrel in the 1990s where these cultural forms were sold off to mainstream audiences by multinational companies who gradually subsumed the smaller independent projects that had been started naïvely in the 1980s (bands, record labels, art, graphics etc.) as a result of a post-punk DIY spirit. As such these signs became divested of their initial meanings and became simple styles that could be applied to any product to confer a certain cache. So the work of Gillian Wearing was ripped off on Volkswagen billboards. The songs of Nirvana became mindless teen-angst anthems; all because they seemed to have the ability to talk to their audiences in a more truthful and direct, one-to-one manner. Perversely, at the same time there was an increasing awareness by these artists and musicians that they were self-consciously generating PRODUCT – Nirvana's ironic song titles, the work of Damien Hirst. The great successes were Channel 4 with its remit to engage with these specialised niche audiences, which of course by the mid-1990s meant that they were attracting exactly the kinds of audiences advertisers wanted to capture. There were the small independent labels like Creation that were eaten up by Sony Records or Miramax which was subsumed by Disney. All because multinational capital had realised that in a new leisured economy the unwieldy corporate structure lagged behind the consumer's need for signs of identity and individualism.

Oppositional forms are recuperated within months in the culture's need to find, chew and spit out novelties. We see my generation's schizophrenic conflation of 1980's-style materialism with old 1960s notions of self-actualisation and enlightenment. And it was multinational corporatism that had the power to weld these together.

Back in the early 1990's, my bus repeatedly took me past a billboard advert for the Halifax Building Society that depicted a house made up of people pulling together to form the walls and roof of a house. I hated this advert with a passion; it really got under my skin. I suppose it was to do with the way it seemed to address a wide constituency (me and everyone on the bus, the commuters in their huddled masses going to work) with images of cooperation and solidarity, images of a society pulling together to produce constructive work; a naïve utopian dream of building a society on mutual cooperation. Ironically, this was at the same time the Halifax became a bank and was floated on the stock exchange. It seemed to me the most dishonest advert I'd seen. Advertising does not seek to bring people together in cooperation but as John Berger presciently points out in *Ways of Seeing*, it makes them rivals, it goes to make them envious of each other as well as to make the 'working self envious of the consuming self'. It seeks to 'steal the consumer's love of herself as she is and sell it back to her for the price of the product.' All the rest is a sham to make the consumer feel good about their investment, to make them bask in the glow of some utopian vision of mutual cooperation. These were images of the 'welfare state', right at the moment when private money was funnelling into the NHS, an advert for mortgage services at the moment that more houses were re-possessed than ever before. Advertising like this was seeking to obliterate the context, to create an endlessly deferred future, to make history mythical.

The contradictions have always been there. At a time when global capital threatens to sweep all before it through its need to control markets and territories through price-fixing and political power, the individual has never been so negligible to the corporate boardroom.

Who cares about the individual at the right-wing Clear Channel? And yet the product and its concomitant brand have to pretend to address the single individual as if the communication is some highly personal conversation/dialogue, not the one-sided directive it really is. And it needs the work of designers and filmmakers, artists and musicians to smooth over those contradictions.

So we arrive here where the progress of global capital has perversely restricted choice. It has made the street – the high street – a boring, anodyne, homogenised place, the same shops, the same cafes. Most cities seem to have eradicated their pasts. They have destroyed that memory and replaced it with what? A kind of hyperspace. A 'phantasmagoria' of space to establish the city centre as a kind of 'pleasure park' of consumption, to make consumption an innocent and sanctified thing, to cut consumption off from the production of the goods.

It has worked on me. Maybe it has worked too well. I have been suckered by the way these companies address me, as an atomised 30-something male, with a wife and two kids (semi-educated, design-conscious). I am encouraged to buy into this lifestyle, to believe that what I buy is meaningful, defines me, and says something about me. But I want to make real decisions (you know, my busy, busy life... means I'll take those shortcuts through to feeling unique.) I am encouraged to see myself as an individual whose only relationship to other people is based on envy and a sense of what I lack but corporate capitalism can't deal with me as a real individual with a history, with weaknesses and irrational fears, with strange enthusiasms. It can only see me in terms of demographics, in terms of a bunch of lifestyle decisions. I am not a lifestyle; I am more than a sum of what I buy. The new-city street makes me feel like my whole life has been art-directed. Everything put on a plate, crediting me with no time, no imagination to find what will be meaningful to me. I look

around and I think it's because I've settled into 30-something complacency. Now it feels everything is happening somewhere else, behind closed doors by committee.

As a result the city street itself has become branded, flayed, a shadow sheared away from what it used to represent. There is no culture to draw from, or at least it is thoroughly marginalised. There are no margins to operate in anymore. In a city like Leeds there is a new kind of pseudo-street called the Light, a covered street, not an arcade, which neuters the street, makes it a safe and controllable museum-piece to shop in, spend leisure time in. Nothing surprising or inappropriate will happen here. It's an empty space like the rest of the city centre: a hollow spectacle, a vaulted cathedral of commerce. I walk the escalators and feel light-headed, a kind of post-modern Stendahl's syndrome. Here it is. Isolated, seamless, consecrated ground, it becomes increasingly difficult to relate the products sold to the conditions of their production.

The irony of this of course is that the more homogenous this city centre becomes, perhaps the more people will become bored. If everything looks the same they will look for difference. If we really are individuals, as the adverts seem to suggest, then we might just go and do unpredictable things.

Drunken fights still occur. There is violence and crime and racism here still. A city like Leeds is still a northern provincial city with its problems of pissed-up lads looking for a scrap. Under the surface, the same tensions exist. These threaten to explode the new myths of the city (it's interesting to note New Labour's anti-social behaviour orders, as well as its recent demonisation of 'binge-drinking culture').

In the recent Woodgate and Bowyer court case in Leeds, it was significant to see how city centre violence (racist or not) was dealt with. Like football's gentrification, the problems have simply been relocated outside the football ground or to the out of town estates and the kind of hysterical moral panic engendered by the media by this court case and by recent football hooliganism displays a real fear that these contradictions may just resurface and explode the myth of the safe football ground or the city centre as separate from the rest of the city (when we know that the bars that define it as the mythic '24-hour city' have a close relationship with drug money coming from outside the city centre, from the 'sub-class' hinterlands). In fact football's gentrification reflects these wider developments. Again, they have priced the working-class fan out of the equation. The game is run by PLCs, taken out of our hands and into the bank vaults of shareholders: repackaged and sold back to us as entertainment (no, for most fans, it clearly is not entertainment; it can be too painful). We cannot deal with disappointment anymore. (When kids play 'pass the parcel' everyone wins now.) Sometimes your team loses. Sometimes it struggles. Where are our lives, caught between this disappointment and the money and emotion we invest in them? We are promised what can never really be delivered.

So the Council can increase the CCTV cameras to paper over the widening gap between rich and poor, attempt to patrol and control the spaces. They can ban fly-posting or create official fly-posting drums but there are still gang wars over these spaces. Fly-posters have been threatened and assaulted by these gangs. But the official sites are patrolled and controlled. Permission is sought and given. All the rest doesn't exist.

In the 19th century, city centres had slaughterhouses. People were not squeamish about seeing the process of production, seeing how the meat got to the table. The product's brand goes to dress up the relations of production, to finally cut it free from its past. But finally what we repress comes back to haunt us. This process of separation started

ironically with Le Corbusier and his urban schemes, *Plan Voisin* and *la Ville Radieuse*. Le Corbusier wanted to eradicate completely 'the street corridor'. Perhaps it was simply too messy for him, it didn't fit into his rational utopian dreams. There were no half measures; the city would be zoned and its functions separated. Residential zones would be linked to commercial and industrial districts by highways that crossed manicured English gardens. There was no place for the street in this plan. It seems ironic now because Le Corbusier's dream was predominantly socialist and leftwing in character and he was threatening to destroy the very location of revolution – the street.

The street has always had these connotations: the cross-pollination of different classes and ideas; the chance of assembly and political violence and the sense that all revolutions started on the street. Was Le Corbusier's dream the same as Hausmann's in Paris? To make the city street a controllable space for the purposes of function/circulation rather than for Hausmann's predominantly militaristic and commercial purposes? Was this the equivalent of Marx's prediction of the state withering away under Communism? Would the street also wither in the new socialist state? Poets like Mayakovsky in Russia and the Italian Futurists like Balla with his The *Street Enters the House* eulogised the street as the scene of political insurrection. They sang songs to the barricades. This was revisited by the students of May 1968, and in particular by the situationists' surrealist proclamations that 'poetry is in the streets, under the pavement the beach..'

Le Corbusier's ideas of course were extremely influential in post-war Britain, with typically back-handed attempts, particularly in the late 1950s and early 1960s. An interesting curio, the 'Poster of the Future' suggests how the poster site might be used in a new post-Buchanan report city centre (traffic away from pedestrianised districts).

At the same time, it's interesting that the idea of the street was reappraised by the Smithsons in their plans for both Park Hill Flats in Sheffield and for their planned reconstruction of Coventry. There was a sense of attempting to maintain the fabric of street life within a modernist framework – allowing the kind of communal activities that existed in the working class city street. Was there a kind of nostalgia already for what was seen as the working class street? Was this a sign that it was already on the wane around the time of *Coronation Street* and a *Taste of Honey*? Was this a part of the Independent Group's strange combination of technophilia and nostalgia? (I love the Smithsons' photo-montages of Park Hill street decks with Jimmy Dean and Marilyn Monroe skulking in the shadowy corners).

Perhaps it was in Jane Jacobs' *The Death and Life of Great American Cities* that a fully articulated defence of the street began. This reacted to Le Corbusier's ideas by advocating Greenwich Village as a role model of urban living, with its mixed uses, its streets patrolled by concerned eyes, a dynamic and vital cultural street life.

Writers such as Richard Sennett in the *Fall of Public Man* and *Conscience of the Eye* who saw a strange kind of order in the confusion and heterogeneity of the city street added to these observations. Similarly Kevin Lynch contrasted his vision of the city happening on a small scale, at street level with the god-like planners in City Hall. His concerns were primarily with the 'imageability of the city' and this was managed at street level. De Certeau in his *Walking in New York* shared a similar agenda. In the work of the situationists and such as Colin Rowe in his *Collage City*, the confusion of the city street, with its posters and signs, was a kind of dadaist assemblage, a work of art that could derange the senses through strange collisions and jump-cuts.

This rude, dynamic vital street culture has always equally nourished and repelled a higher culture. We can go back to Victorian days to see the importance of the poster on the street culture of the time – from the circus poster to the handbills/fly-posters routinely advertising hangings, floggings etc. (quotes here from contemporary commentators) It is here that concerns over mass literacy through successive education acts and the advance of social democratic movements and political unrest are articulated. The street becomes a sign of a corrupt mass society. In the East End we see Jack the Ripper, extreme poverty and the volatile atmosphere of Brick Lane, all reflected in the history of the poster and the mass illustrated broadsheet. In fact this low form has been something of a distorted mirror to the advance of history. It's possible to read an entire social and political history through the history of the poster (are we at the end of history? is there no mass society anymore that can be addressed with these graphic forms?)

Later in the 20th century, we can talk about the poster in terms of its importance to the hippie underground of course - all that 'hapdash' kind of rubbish. Was the hippie underground a true street culture? Certainly the Notting Hill/Portobello scene of the late 1960s sees a thriving street scene supported by a vital poster culture. Cultural commentators like Dick Hebdige refused hippie as an authentic street culture, regarding it as a primarily middle-class phenomenon. Does this mean that this was the new déclassé middle-classes who had fallen out of their class through drugs, bohemia whatever, attempting to colonise the street? Jonathan Raban's *Soft City* attempts to sketch this kind of city. He talks about the street as a 'theatre of signs' that eclipses signs of class and taste. The poster is part of that network of communication.

Aspects of this counter-culture of the late 1960s ironically set up forms of distribution and ways of doing things

that punk fastened onto in the late seventies. The posters of Jamie Reid act as the go-between here. Punk was a contrived semi-genuine street culture – however those streets were on New York's lower east side, not the Kings Road. *Fucked Up and Photocopied* is a testament to the street culture of the late 1970s and early 1980s at a time when a genuine street culture coming from New York, hip-hop was emerging. Central to this culture was the idea of the block party as a *gesamt-kunstwerk* encompassing a number of different cultural activities from emceeing to graffiting to riding bikes. Are all these forms artworks in themselves – do the participants in these subcultures act as 'living posters' that spectacularly interrupt the common-sense signifiers of the everyday life? Dick Hebdige and others regard this as a subversive art act – the heavily artificial and coded communication of difference in the city street, acting as a kind of surrealist montage/bricolage of commonplace elements in new, transgressive forms. Are these resisting politically the invitations of the billboard, the appeal to common-sense values of settling down with two kids with a mortgage and a steady job?

Have all the subsequent subcultures been just diluted versions of these two vital cultural expressions? Indeed it's interesting that these are the only subcultures to uphold the original spirit of rock'n roll, as an adolescent dissenting voice against all the invitations of the grown-up world. However even these subcultures have been commodified more or less. Recently, Nike produced a series of posters for the 2002 World Cup portraying a number of well-known football stars in a distinctive stencil-style, using a graphic language derived from 1968 Situationism, from *Atelier Populaire*, punk and hip-hop; from oppositional to mainstream. Style and design sheared away from the political and the ethical, neutered and tamed. Advertising obliterates history. I wonder if this poster campaign was specifically British as I feel we have increasingly

come to see ourselves as professional style merchants, exporting that invisible cargo called 'cool' as a series of post-modern empty vessels across the world: a plethora of styles to sell the products of a new commodity culture with. We are now supposed to be beyond bare subsistence and need to buy things to affirm our sense of ourselves in this new confusing, surrealist, jump-cut world of strange signifiers and meanings. Our way out of course is through advertising.

Which leads us straight back to where we were at the start.

Where does this get us? The poster has been a sign of a street culture for more than a century. Nowadays of course, the poster is seen to advertise exactly that culture of bars and clubs, of rock n roll and modernity. In a city like Leeds where a vision of urban blight is the number of 'to let' signs littering whole neighbourhoods and billboards selling products to a car-bound consumer, the poster at least stands for a vital spontaneous, responsive and dynamic popular culture. OK we might decry that culture now as too passive and commodified but this isn't really the point. Perhaps people still use that culture in interesting and idiosyncratic ways. They access that culture in interesting ways and it seems like a poorer culture where there is no cross-fertilisation of ideas/signs/images: where each audience is clearly demarcated the options that are made for them – okay, I'm not a fan of hardcore techno but I want to walk down the street and see a poster that invites me persuasively and effectively to join in that culture. I'm not a theatre-goer but I want the option of seeing what's on so that I feel like the whole of this culture is genuinely open to me if I so demand it, not just the small parcel of culture that is supposed to be mine because I am a white middle-class bloke in my thirties. My most memorable and formative experiences came about through those kind of accidental meetings with cultures and ideas I had not come across.

The public poster with its wide remit and constituency has been the gateway to that culture. It would seem a much poorer culture where those accidental and fortuitous communications are lost in the increasing specialisation and fragmentation of the audience.

Aidan Winterburn was born in 1968 and lives in Wakefield, Yorkshire with his wife and two sons. He now teaches, Critical and Contextual Studies, at Leeds Metropolitan University. He was a part of the band Edsel Auctioneer, scriptwriter for many short films, co-founder of a video workshop and lecturer on art, architecture and film history at Doncaster College. He edits the magazines *Spliced* and *Politics Is a Matter of Tracking and Kerning*.

Noa Szgal, Emek-Yezreel College, Israel

The Images Publishing Group of Melbourne, Australia, and the author, Malcolm Frost, invited graphic design students to design posters to promote this book. The results of this competition are published in the preceding pages.

*Street Talk* discusses the possibility of the conventional printed public poster succeeding against alternative media (the Internet etc.), the accusation that posters are now part of urban blight, and whether the frenetic urban realm (both visually and environmentally) means that the poster has lost its power and effectiveness.

The visual defence of the poster is shown, in the main, with groups of posters that are 'cultural', that is, they have been designed for architects, the ballet, opera, cinema, art, exhibitions and literary affairs. They were all used in the public domain. The alternative reality is supplied by texts, talking about the history of the poster, its success and failure, the advance of the new media and the misgivings we all have about the rotting urban fabric.

The authors would like to send kind regards, special wishes and congratulations to Roni Darin, Eugenie Dodd and all the students from Emek-Yezreel College, Israel, for their huge contribution to this book.

The care and professionalism taken over the presentation of the students' work was wonderful.

Considering the distance between London and the Yezreel Valley and the tight deadline, the staff and students deserve special mention on their fine ability to communicate to complete strangers. (Communication students certainly throughout the UK, should be taught the profound idea of being able to clearly communicate over distance).

We wish the Emek-Yezreel students a brilliant future career and hope all of them continue as practitioners, and that they emerge as giants in our industry.

A new book from Images Publishing Group

aristide
BRUANT
dans
son caba

STREET TALK
The Rise And Fall of the Poster

THE IMAGES
PUBLISHING GROUP
IMAGES HOUSE,
6 BASTOW PLACE
MULGRAVE,
VICTORIA 3170,
AUSTRALIA
TELEPHONE
+613 9561 5544
FAX
+613 9561 4860
EMAIL
books@images.com.au
STREET TALK
THE RISE AND FALL
OF THE POSTER
EXTENT
256 pages
FORMAT
300 x 223 mm
full colour throughout,
case bound, with
over 300 illustrations

BOU
OX

POST NO BILLS

NO
RKING
DO NOT
ENTER
NO STOPPING
W AWAY
ZONE
No access for
unauthorised
persons

STREET TALK

THE RISE AND FALL OF THE POSTER

A NEW BOOK FROM IMAGES PUBLISHING GROUP

256 PAGES, 300 mmx223mm PAGE SIZE

FULL COLOUR THROUGHOUT

CASE-BOUND WITH OVER 300 ILLUSTRATIONS

THE IMAGES PUBLISHING GROUP

IMAGES HOUSE, 6 BASTOW PLACE

NULGRAVE, VICTORIA 3170, AUSTRALIA

TEL +613 9561 5544

FAX +61 3 9561 4860

EMAIL BOOKS@IMAGES.COM.AU

Hi

Inbar Miara
Adi Betman

Take the 6 train, which goes out every 17 minutes, to Astor Place station. Get off at 14 east street and take a 15 minute walk to 1st avenue, to see the antique 4 to 6 stories buildings. Don't miss 7th street, where more than 6000 Japanese immigrants made it their home. And you've got to catch the 268 east 10th street Bathing House (the 5 train has a station there); The number is 212-6749250 (call between 9 in the morning and 10 pm). Ticket costs 19 $, but it's just great! If you're hungry, go to 302 east 12 street to John's, where for 10 $ you get a full meal (the place was established 80 years ago!). In the shops in the corner of 105th street and 2nd avenue there are cool 1/2 minutes from there there's the beautiful 480 square feet Thompikns park. Now I'll have to be brief, 'cause the cell rates are 29 $ for 99 minutes, and I should've been back 10 minutes ago:

# Street Talk
## The Rise and Fall of the Poster

The Images Publishing Group
Image House, 6 Bastow Place
Mulgrave, Victoria 3170
Australia
T +613 9561 5544
F +613 9561 4860
E books@images.com.au

256 pages
300mm X 223mm page size
full colour throughout
case bound
with over 300 illustrations

Sharon Mets

Maxim Litvak          Dana Appleboum

Street Talk

A new
book
from
images
Publishing
Group

The Rise
and Fall
of the Poster

THE•IMAGES•PUBLISHING•GROUP•
IMAGES•HOUSE•6•BASTOW•PLACE
MULGRAVE•VICTORIA•3170••
AUSTRALIA••
TEL+613 9561 5544••
FAX+613 9561 4860••
E MAIL BOOKS@IMAGES.COM.AU••
256 PAGES  300MM x 223MM•FORMAT
FULL•COLOUR•THROUGHT••
CASE•BOUND••
WITH•OVER•300•ILLUSTRATION••

NO BEAT TO NO BEAT NO BEAT TO NO BE

NO BEAT! TO NO BLACK
TRRRRRRRRR..
UFF!
BEAT!
BEAT!

WOWW!!!
BEEEP!!!!!!!
KRANCH
NOCKNOCKNOC

STREET
TALK
THE RISE
AND FALL
OF THE
POSTER

A NEW BOOK FROM
IM-KEST PUBLISHING GROUP

Liat Taub

Karin Koren

The Rise

and

Fall

of the

Poster

Efrat Ben-Ezra
Zeev Mendelovich
Anat Tel

Sharon Ayalon

**StreetTalk**

A new book from Images Publishing Group

256 pages, 300mm x 223mm page size,
full colour throughout, case-bound,
with over 300 illustrations

**The**
**Rise**
**and**
**Fall**
**of the**
**Poster**

**The Images Publishing Group**

Images House
6 Bastow Place, Mulgrave
Victoria 3170
Australia
t  +613 9561 5544
f  +613+9561 4860
e  books@images.com.au

Tali Mina

street talk
The Rise
And Fall
Of The Poster
A NEW BOOK FROM
IMAGES PUBLISHING
GROUP 256 PAGES, 300mm x 223mm PAGE SIZE,
FULL COLOUR THROUGHOUT, CASE - BOUND,
WITH OVER 300 ILLUSTRATIONS.
THE IMAGES PUBLISHING GROUP,
IMAGES HOUSE, 6 BASTOW PLACE,
MULGRAVE ,VICTORIA 3170, AUSTRALIA.
TEL +613 9561 5544
FAX +613 9561 4860
EMAIL books@images.com.au

191

Sophiya Sayag    Michal Ziv

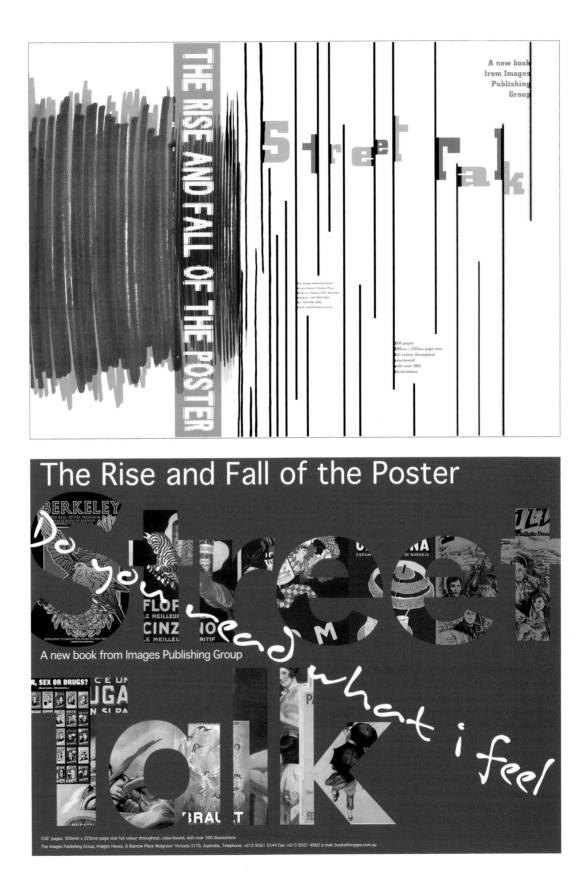

Meytal Yair

Idan Heskia
Moran Fogel

# STREET TALK

THE RISE AND FALL OF THE POSTER

256 pages
300mm x 223mm
page size
full colour throughout
case bound
with over
300 illustrations

The Images Publishing Group Mulgrave, Victoria 3170, Australia

A new book from Images Publishing Group

telephone +613 9561 5544
fax +613 9561 6860
e-mail books@images.com.au

"FOR THE SINGLE BRICK, SHALL CRY OUT FROM THE WALL" FROM HABAKKUK, ONE OF THE BOOKS OF THE OLD TESTAMENT BIBLE

THE HISTORIAN OF ANY CITY RUNS PARALLEL WITH A HISTORY OF PUBLIC SIGNS, SINCE TIME BEGAN

FOR CENTURIES PEOPLE HAVE WRITTEN THEIR NAMES, INITIALS OR MESSAGES ON ANY SURFACE, WITH ANY COARSE INSTRUMENT, ANYWHERE INTO THE FABRIC OF THE CITY.

HUMAN GESTURES HAVE CLEARLY COMMUNICATED A VARIETY OF EMOTIONS, DIRECTIONS, QUALITATIVE JUDGEMENTS AND SO ON. IT'S IMPOSSIBLE TO LEGISLATE AGAINST PUBLIC GESTURES BECAUSE WE HAVE CREATED A UNIVERSAL LANGUAGE OF APPROVAL AND DISAPPROVAL, CONTEMPT AND SUPERSTITION (LIKE SPITTING ON THE GROUND TO BRING US LUKE).

"IF YOU'RE GOING TO BE AROUND ALL THE TIME, YOU'D BETTER PUT YOUR NAME UP" A GRAFFITI ARTIST SAID TO IAIN SINCLAIR, INTREPID CITY WALKER AND INVESTIGATOR.

THESE ABANDONED MESSAGES SEEM TO BE THE CITY SPEAKING TO ITSELF.

THE PUBLIC POSTER RECEIVES ONLY TOKEN INTEREST NOW,

"KILROY WOS ERE"

CITIES HAVE ALWAYS BEEN PLACES OF CIVIC DEMONSTRATION

AS EVERY ABOVE GROUND UNDERGROUND AND IN THE HEAVENS. ALDOUS HUXLEY IN "BRAVE NEW WORLD"

STREET TALK
THE RISE AND THE FALL OF THE POSTER
A NEW BOOK FROM IMAGES PUBLISHING GROUP

Lior Mastey
Keren Betman

Yael Rosenzwieg

Verticals horizontals

lines of time and space

starting then stopping          structures

Grids        and

Taking off and landing

# STREET

## TALK

in the street

Blank faces

### The rise and fall of the poster

Why are they in such a rush

Concrete and metal

Street after street

Person after person

buildings towering overhead          Guided by invisible lines

hidden

For the masses below

messages

Here                    and there

neon

map

Below my feet

abandoned

messages

labyrinth of signs

Past

constant movement

read      the      street

## A new book from Images Publishing Group

256 pages,          300mm x 223mm page size, full colour throughout,

case-bound,          with over 300 illustrations.

Jonathan Bourne & Victoria Legg

# STREET TALK
## THE RISE AND FALL OF THE POSTER

A new book from Images publishing group.
256 pages, 300mm x 223mm page size,
full colour throughout, case-bound,
with over 300 illustrations.

'Stop the traffic' graphics...

Images Publishing Group
Images House
6 Bastow Place
Mulgrave
Victoria
3170
Australia

Tel: +613 9561 5544    Fax: +613 9561 4860    E-mail: books@images.com.au

Daniel Evans

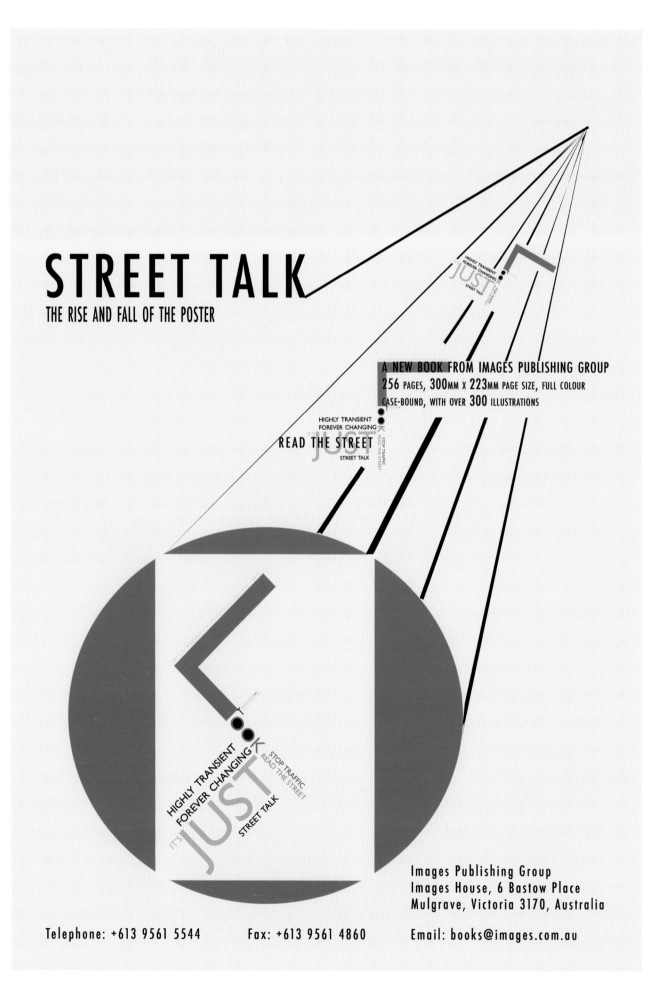

Kirsten Elliott

Harry Edmonds

A new book from
Images Publishing Group

With over 300 illustrations
Full colour throughout
256 pages and case-bound
Page size: 300mm x 223mm

The Images Publishing Group
Images House, 6 Bastow Place
Mulgrave, Victoria 3170, Australia

T: +613 9561 5544
F: +613 9561 4860
E: books@images.com.au

The rise and fall of the poster

street
talk

Miguel Bravo

Helen O'Byrne    Seema Dhah

STREET TALK

The
Rise
and
Fall
of
the
Poster

A new book from Images publishing Group.

The Images Publishing Group
Images House,
6 Bastow Place,
Mulgrave,
Victoria 3170
Australia

Telephone +613 9561 5544
Fax +613 9561 4860
email: books@images.com.au

256 pages, 300 mm × 2233 mm page size,
full colour throughout, case bound,
with over 300 illustrations.

Jasminder Matharo

STREET TALK.
the rise and fall
of the poster

A new book from Images Publishing Group

Jo Hooker

Robert Bootle

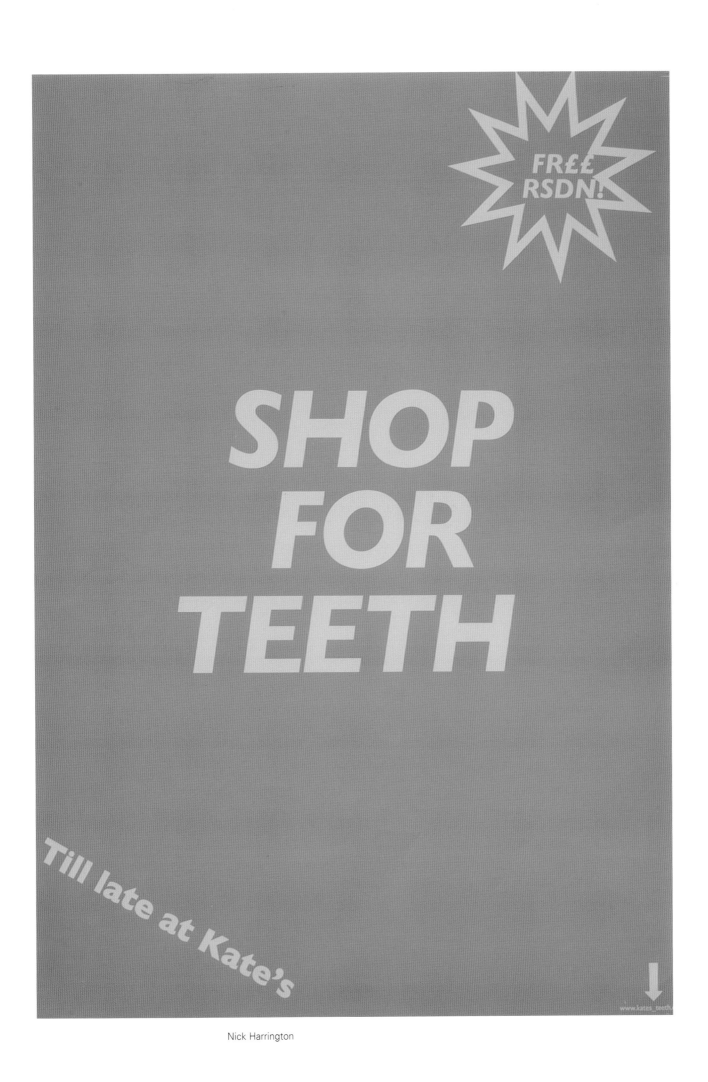

Nick Harrington

# Street Talk

## The Rise and Fall of the Poster

Bryony Matthewman

I like fly-posting and the
general urban graffiti mess.
It's like a public
information service.

**Diran Adebayo**
Author and commentator
**Photograph Gerry Mitchell**
London 2005

Society drives people crazy
with lust and calls it advertising.

**John Lahr**
American critic and writer
**Photograph Gina Moriaty**
London 2005

We are anthill people
upon an anthill world.

**Ray Bradbury**
American writer
**Photograph Jesus Sierra**
Shoreditch London 2005

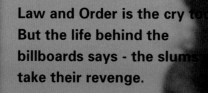

**Law and Order is the cry today**
**But the life behind the**
**billboards says - the slums**
**take their revenge.**

**Nelson Algren**
American writer
**Photograph Gina Moriaty**
Central London 2005

MAIDEN

Sometimes it seems that it is not possible to do more than reflect the decay around and within us, than sing sad and bitter songs of disillusion and defeat.

**RD Laing**
Psychiatrist and poet
**Photograph Gerry Mitchell**
London 2005

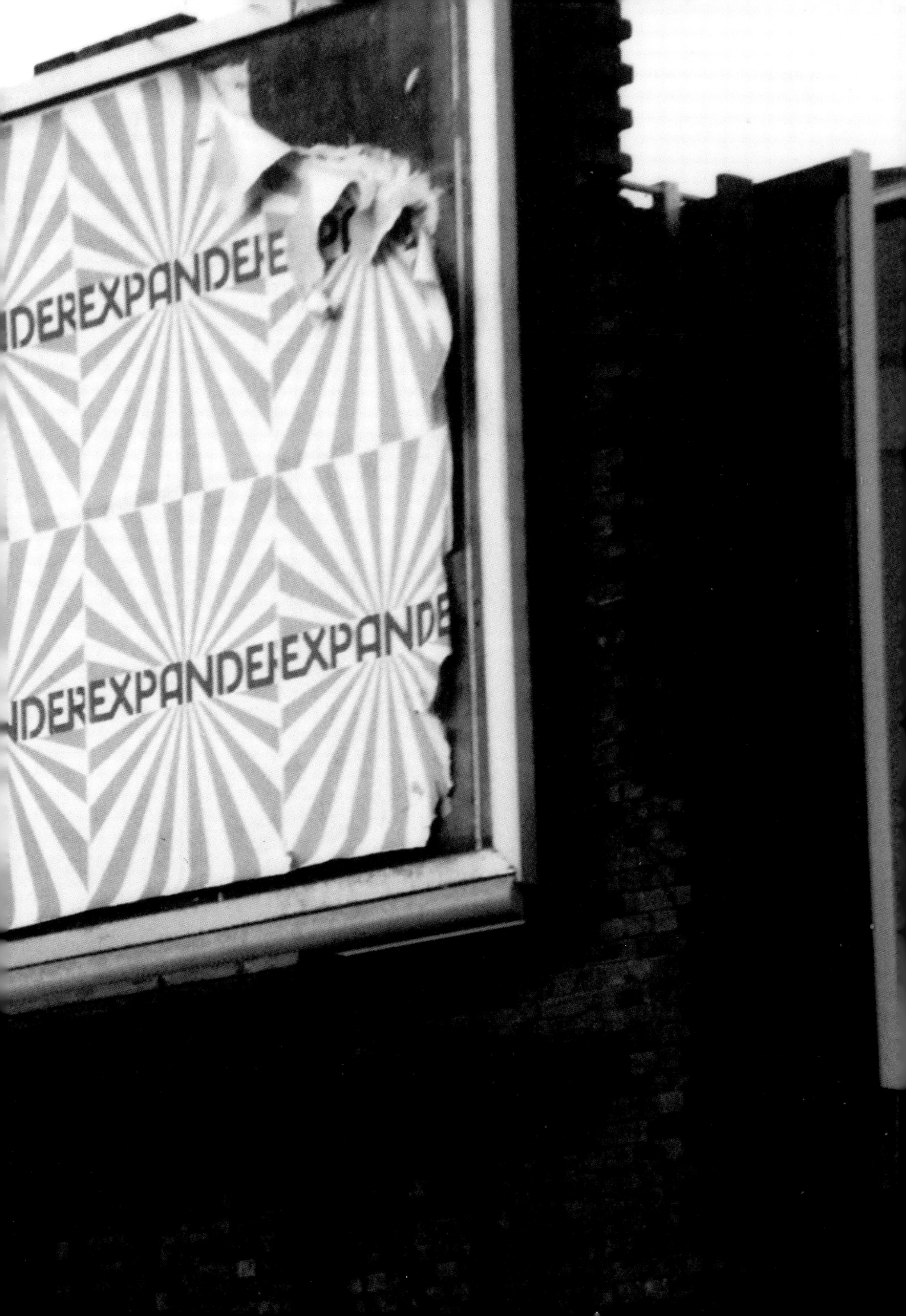
NDEREXPANDERE
NDEREXPANDEREXPANDE

I love this dirty old town.

**Clifford Odets**
**Ernest Lehman**
Sweet Smell of Success
United Artists 1957
**Photograph Paolo Rosselli**
Barcelona 2003

The books listed below are those we
have referred to most often, and we
thank the authors and publishers for
their help, information and inspiration.
Publications on The Poster is a huge
slice of the art and design industry and
would be impossible here to describe in
any worthwhile sense. Some museums
hold large collections which the general
public can look through, some galleries
sell cheap reproductions, auction houses
often sell historic originals. But one can
easily obtain (usually for free) posters
that you find interesting by applying to
the designer, client and/or the printer.

100+3 Swiss Posters
Siegfried Odermatt
Wager Verlag Zurich

History of Photography
Ian Jeffrey
World of Art
Thames and Hudson

The book of saints
Bulfinch Press
Little, Brown and Company

Manet to Toulouse-Lautrec
French lithographs
British Museum Publications

London the biography
Peter Ackroyd
Chatto and Windus

A history of the Dutch poster
Pieter Brattinga
Otterlo 1968

Poster Design
Tom Eckersley
London 1954

Japanese posters and prints
Ikko Tanaka
Kyoto 1976

Hans Schleger - a life of design
Pat Schleger
Lund Humphries 2001

Images of an Era:
the American Poster 1945-75
Smithsonian Institution

Identity Kits:
a pictorial survey of visual signals
Germano Facetti and Alan Fletcher
Studio Vista London

Dictionary of Bibliography
Cambridge University Press

Sources of Modern Architecture
a critical bibliography
Dennis Sharp
Granada Publishing

Architecture in Photography
Paolo Rosselli
Skira Editore Milan

Santiago Calatrava
Dennis Sharp
E & FN Spon London

The Beggarstaff Posters
Colin Campbell
Barrie & Jenkins London

Kisho Kurokawa at RIBA
Dennis Sharp
BookArt London

History of Posters
John Bardicoat
World of Art
Thames and Hudson

Connell Ward and Lucas
Dennis Sharp
BookArt London

History of the Poster
Josef and Shizuko Muller-Brockmann
Phaidon Press Limited

Roman Cieslewicz
Margo Rouard-Snowman
Thames and Hudson

A Visual History of
20th century Architecture
Dennis Sharp
Images Publishing Group

### Acknowledgments:

Malcolm Frost and Angharad Lewis would like to thank, wholeheartedly, the photographers who have been involved in this project : Jesus Sierra and Lucy Sierra, Gerry Mitchell and Gina Moriaty, Catherine Slessor, Paolo Rosselli and his publisher Skira Editore Milan, Jilly Shaw and Steven Gill. They have recorded for us the blight of our times in : New York City, Buenos Aires, Leicester, Berlin, Paris, Milan, Madrid, Barcelona, Dublin, Rome, Amsterdam, Venice, Florence, Shanghai, Antwerp, San Francisco, Toronto, Los Angeles, London and Tenerife.

We especially thank all the designers whose waking hours are, not only, subject to crummy urban environments but also have to contend with the phenomena in their working, professional lives and who have freely contributed to this book :Design Workshop, Canada; Pentagram, London; Massimo Vignelli; Bob Gill; The Estate of Abram Games; Experimental Jetset, Amsterdam; Malone Design, London; Erosie, Eindhoven; Alon Levin, London; A2/SW/HK, London; Value and Service, London; Kerr/Noble, London; Jonathan Ellery/Browns, London; Jonathan Barnbrook, London; and Constantin Demner, London.

Without the patience and outstanding work of Graeme Martin of Igma Imaging this book would not have seen the light of day. Without the support of Alessina Brooks and Paul Latham at Images Publishing the project would not have got off the ground. We are eternally grateful for their tenacity and encouragement, and send our warmest regards to all our friends in Melbourne, Australia.

WHITCOMB
COURT WC2
CITY OF WESTMINSTER

JERRY
Springer
the opera
THE MULTI AWARD WINNING MUSICAL
HALF PRICE THEATRE TICKETS →

**Tout passe**
everything passes
**Tout casse**
everything perishes
**Tout lasse**
everything palls